Your Life Only a Gazillion Times Better

Your Life
only a Gazillion times better

A Practical Guide to Creating the Life of Your Dreams

Cathy Breslin
Judy May Murphy

Health Communications, Inc.
Deerfield Beach, Florida

www.bcibooks.com

Library of Congress Cataloging-in-Publication Data

Breslin, Cathy
    Your life only a gazillion times better : a practical guide to creating the life of
your dreams / Cathy Breslin, Judy May Murphy.
        p. cm.
    Includes bibliographical references.
    ISBN 0-7573-0246-7
    1. Self-actualization (Psychology) I. Murphy, Judy May. II. Title.

    BF637.S4B734 2005
    646.7—dc22

                                                                        2005046315

Publisher: Health Communications, Inc.
              3201 S.W. 15th Street
              Deerfield Beach, FL 33442-8190

Cover design by Larissa Hise Henoch
Inside book design by Lawna Patterson Oldfield

To my father, Daniel Breslin,
my inspiration.

—CATHY

To Danny Breen and Tom Tully,
true friends are golden.

—JUDY MAY

Acknowledgments

We would like to thank Ishana Leonard and Mari Smith, James Ferguson, Joanna Kennedy, Pam Gibbons, Gary and Ruth Ailes, Linda Kedy, Kathy Weidenbaum, Loren Slocum, the TR crew, Rogie Robinson, Sandy Oulwek, Shannon McLoren, Sally Vail, Tina Zeigler, Brian Martin, Sue Wiggins, Sonni Kane, John Burgess, Vicki St George, Jan G. Filip, Pamela Harmon, Jan Walker, Jeff Roberti, Gabby Giffords, Hal Taylor, Bobby Ruiz, Callie O'Brien, Emma Glackin, Michael Morningstar, Tammy Hair, and Mary Allen.

Our hearts and thanks are with our friends and mentors at Rich Dad Poor Dad, Michael Lechter, Sharon Lechter, Bob Weidenbaum, and Robert and Kim Kiyosaki. We are also blessed to have such a wonderful team at HCI and would especially like to thank Tom Sand for discovering us and our editor Amy Hughes for all her wonderful guidance.

Contents

Icon Key

Belief

Breaking the Old Pattern

Practical Dreaming

Foreword

Smile from Within

Who Am I?

I am a mother, wife, daughter, sister, friend, business owner, business partner, writer, philanthropist and volunteer. For most of my life, when I was asked the question, "Who are you?" my answer would be couched in the form of one or more of these labels, or simply, "All of the above. I wear a lot of hats."

Each one of these categories describes who I am *in relation to someone else*. As a wife, I am Michael's partner in life. I am Phillip, Shelly and Rick's mother. I am my parents' daughter . . . and the pattern continues. These labels describe my interpersonal relationships. Over the years I have become quite comfortable defining myself by identifying these relationships. I have found my greatest joy and sense of accomplishment and self-worth through seeing myself as a wife, mother, business owner, etc.

Take a moment and answer the question "Who am I?" for yourself. How many hats do you wear?

~ ~ ~

It was not too many years ago that I realized I was using these "hats" as a way to avoid looking further. I was hiding behind the labels. They were not really hats; I would define them more accurately as masks. They create a safe space, a comfort zone, where I can identify myself through the eyes of others. I tend to judge myself by how good a wife I am, how good a mother I am. At times I feel like I have a split personality, because I need to wear several masks at the same time. How can I be all things to all people? Do you ever feel this way?

Have you ever caught yourself in the middle of changing masks? I will find myself on a business call and see the second phone line ringing. I quickly finish the first business call and promptly answer the second in my business voice. In the split second when I realize it is my son, my whole presence changes, and I become a mom. I can hear my voice and tone transform automatically.

When I first read *Your Life Only a Gazillion Times Better* it hit me between the eyes in the first chapter. The very first exercise asks, "Who are you, physically, emotionally, intellectually?" I was instantly booted out of my comfort zone. I couldn't figure out where to use "mother, wife, daughter and so on." I had to look deeper within myself. It took me back in time.

Several years ago, our son was having problems. It was the most difficult period of my life. I was devastated. I was drowning in guilt and feeling like a total failure as a mother. It was difficult to even get out of bed in the morning. Fortunately, our son entered a program that included parenting seminars as part of its curriculum. Michael and I attended in hopes of becoming better parents and finding a way to help our son.

Were we ever surprised! The entire seminar was about us as individuals. The first day the instructor asked, "How can you expect to help your child if you can't help yourself?" For three days we focused on our intrapersonal skills—how we deal with ourselves.

Two of the greatest lessons I have ever learned came out of that seminar. While quite simple and founded in common sense, I believe they hold the key to self-fulfillment and finding true happiness. They are: "You cannot change other people. You can only change yourself and how you react or relate to other people," and "Everything happens for a reason."

You may be reading this book because you picked it up in a bookstore in the airport or because someone gave it to you as a gift. Regardless of how it came to be in your hands, you are reading it for a reason.

This book is a self-guided tour through your mind that will allow you to discover your own brilliance, gifts and dreams, and allow you to plot a course that will help you create the life you want. When I first read the book, my instant reaction was, "I wish I had read it twenty years ago." To acquire the skills outlined in this book is truly a gift that only you can give yourself.

One of my favorite parts of the book is in the second chapter, where it discusses the "shoulds" of life: "Often we buy into an idea of what our life 'should' be like; we think we 'should' follow a certain career path or lifestyle. This mindset (and everyone has one) has overly influenced our choices through the years, often in negative ways."

In my opinion the "shoulds" of life represent our interpretations of what others expect of us, instead of what we want for ourselves. On the flip side, many times we tend to project our "shoulds" on to our children and the people most dear to us.

Define who you are and what your goals are, and work on changing your own self-awareness by embracing the exercises in this book. By defining your dreams and goals, you will bring clarity to who you are and what is really important to you. It is amazing how just writing down your goals can help you start focusing on them—and achieving them!

"Change starts and continues with you"—chapter eight

By improving yourself, through working on your intrapersonal skills and building self-awareness and fulfillment, you will find a wonderful by-product. As a result of feeling better about yourself, your relationships (interpersonal) will automatically improve as well.

I am still studying, learning, practicing, failing and practicing some more every day to work on Sharon. I am proud of myself as a wife, as a mom, as a daughter, as a sister, as a friend, as a business owner, as a business partner, as a writer, as a philanthropist and as a volunteer. My goal is to be proud of Sharon Lechter!

My wish for you is that your life is a gazillion times better. It can start today.

Thank you.
—Sharon Lechter

Give a smile and you shall receive a smile.

Our Stories

Admit it to yourself—you'd like to improve some aspects of your life. Maybe your job isn't all that fulfilling, and you'd like to make a change but don't know where to start. Perhaps you are in a relationship that really doesn't support you in the ways you would like. You may feel like you've hit rock bottom with no where else to turn, or maybe you simply aren't sure what you want out of life and love but know you don't have it now. It could be that you are doing really well and yet you know this isn't the best it could be. If any of these descriptions ring true— you've picked up the right book! Even if you love your life and many aspects of it, we'd be willing to bet there are some (or many) things you would love to change for the better.

We know you don't need long-winded advice, finger-pointing, or experts giving you lists of uncomfortable or impractical things to do to get rich and famous. That's why we've taken a different approach. In this book we have distilled our teachings and methods into short, easy sections that focus on the details of your life and dreams. We've made the book interactive, with specific exercises to help you take control of your life. And we've kept the tone positive and fun throughout. That's right, fun—because only when enjoying yourself while reading this book can you really overhaul your life. This is about actually getting the results you want, not about intellectually knowing what to do.

After helping hundreds of clients find the lives they truly want to live, we are confident in our methods of tackling old habits and patterns of behavior that limit potential and life quality. As life coaches responsible for countless successful transformations and life improvements, we have seen how exciting it can be to make your life a gazillion times better! We have learned how to improve lives dramatically, not just through our professional training, but also because we have seen self-improvement in our own lives and are living examples of how much better one's life can be. No matter what you want to achieve, once you have started to make simple, fast changes to your life, you can easily make your dream life become a reality.

Cathy

As I have found through my personal and professional experience, it is possible to turn your life around and make it better! It took a lot of work, hope and faith to get where I am today, and it wasn't easy by any means, but I made it. After turning my life around, I realized I could teach others how to do the same.

As the eighth child in a family of eleven, I was a happy-go-lucky girl until the age of twelve, when I was diagnosed with a thyroid disease. My life changed dramatically. The disease manifested itself in eye problems and severe mood fluctuations. Throughout my childhood I felt quite disfigured, self-conscious, unattractive and depressed.

At the age of fifteen, I had corrective surgery. After the surgery, I found myself heavier than I had ever been. I wanted to lose the weight, so I began dieting. I became obsessed with my weight and eventually became anorexic. My self-esteem became worse and worse, and in reaction I stopped eating almost entirely. I lived on small amounts of fruit for months at a time and almost lost the battle for life.

All I can remember from this time is that during treatments by professionals I felt isolated and alone. The doctors who treated me saw only my illness. It seemed as though almost every interaction was impersonal and harsh. Specialists and teams of doctors stood around my bed and spoke as if I didn't exist. They used words I couldn't understand and gave me so-called therapy that had long, medical descriptions but very little power to heal me. I felt afraid, insecure and extremely lonely.

At the age of eighteen, due to the anorexia, with the permission of my parents I admitted myself into a psychiatric hospital where I lived on and off for four years. At the deepest part of my depression, I remember a visit from my father, who spoke to me softly and said, "Cathy, you have the inner strength to overcome this problem; you can get through this." With these words resonating in me, I felt inspired to recover for the very first time.

Tragically, a couple of months later my father died, which led me to a horrific setback. As time went on, I realized that nobody else had the resources to give me the help I needed. It finally became apparent to me that I did have the strength—I was the only person who could help me get better. Gradually I began to build my self-confidence, to learn how to eat and how to appreciate myself. During this time I realized that everyone has the strength within to change their lives for the better, a truth that much of this book is based on.

After many years of work, I became healthy and fell in love with life. I found the inner strength that my father had assured me was there. I believe everyone has that same powerful inner strength. Now I have dedicated my life to helping, to teaching other people how they can find strength from within to change their lives permanently. These days I'm a practicing therapist, and I use the lessons I cultivated from years of personal experience through counseling others and teaching self-development skills.

If you face challenges in your life, whether they are large or small, you can always make your life a gazillion times better—no matter what the situation. With our teachings, now gathered in this book, we have shown countless readers how to turn their lives around. It can happen for you, too! This book is the first step in your journey to finding your potential and dreams.

Judy May

I, too, have learned through inspiration, dedication and personal experience how to improve my life, and I have shown many people how to do the same with theirs. My personal experiences gave me a passion and dedication to develop practical, easy techniques to help my clients improve their lives in small and large ways. I, too, have faced many challenges and learned to improve my life despite the obstacles. Many of my discoveries happened when I found strength and inspiration within myself.

My story begins in Dublin, Ireland. When I was eight, my family moved from London to Dublin, and I felt like I left my heart in my childhood home. Unfortunately, I had the disadvantage of underdeveloped muscles in my legs. I couldn't walk properly. In my new school, kids laughed at me. Seeing other kids imitating my unusual gait would make me feel like an outcast. To make matters worse, I was also singled out as the smartest little girl in the class, and that didn't help my popularity. My parents were both working full-time, and I felt that neither of them had time to give me the love and extra support that I craved. I did have some friends, but I mostly retreated into the security of my own little world of books and daydreams about returning to London. I felt abandoned and afraid, and during this time I gradually became very depressed.

The depression would continue in waves during my teenage years, often brought on by some reminder about how my legs were still strange. While in university I started to train as a dancer and managed to completely reverse the muscle problems. However, I still felt alone and frustrated, and I focused on achieving in order to feel worthy of love. At one point, at the age of twenty-one, I was pushing myself so hard that I completely burned out and had a nervous breakdown. I became more depressed than I had been in years.

At the lowest point I stopped eating or sleeping for a couple of days. I was diagnosed as clinically depressed and put on antidepressants by a psychiatrist. For the next ten years, I coped with this awful, debilitating depression by achieving academically and incessantly traveling in search of a home. To others I looked as if I were living a great life, but inside I felt wretched. When things got really bad, I would go back to a doctor to get different, stronger medication.

The final straw came when I was staying in Los Angeles, and a boyfriend dumped me a couple of days before Christmas. I started to self-medicate, swallowing up to five times my prescribed doses. I knew something had to change. An enormous strength appeared from within, and I decided that I would do whatever it took to change my life for the better. I decided to return to Ireland to learn how to be happy again. My search took me around the world once more, often to attend self-help seminars where I learned the skills that healed me and allow me to help heal others. Since then I have been devoted to helping others improve their lives, and my own life is now amazing.

These days I'm a success coach, dividing my time between working in many different countries and developing educational and entertaining television shows. Through my personal experience, I have discovered that across the different aspects of your life (job, family, relationship, wealth, health and daily challenges) there are basic, practical steps you can take toward getting the life you really aspire to. Cathy and I have developed a program that will vastly improve the quality of your life, ensure your emotional stability, and help you achieve your dreams and discover what you truly want. Whether you've had an experience similar to the depression and aloneness we felt in our lives, have had tragedy strike and don't know where else to turn, feel trapped in your life and the choices you've made, or simply, like us, know there are ways to create a better life even if your life is wonderful now—this book is for you.

No matter where you are in your life, how much money you make, how happy you are in your job or how strong your relationships, we believe—in fact, we know—that you can always make your life a gazillion times better!

In the following chapters, we have all sorts of exercises that require your participation. As you go through the book, allow yourself to become active and engaged. We urge you to take the time to do the exercises. Many of them ask you to write down your thoughts. Although there is space to write in the book, for those who like to write a little more, purchase a notebook and use that as you go through the book. We promise that if you put in the effort to be an active participant in this book, you'll get more out it!

1

Discovery

Who Are You?

Many people presume they know who they are, while others are either unsure of who they are or are absolutely sure they don't have a clue as to who they really are and what they're doing on this planet at all. This chapter is all about discovering, or rediscovering, who you are now and who you ultimately want to be.

In school, teachers often asked, "*What* do you want to be when you leave here?" instead of asking, "*Who* do you want to be?"

Just think about it! We spend our lives trying to better our situations, whereas the trick is to improve *who* we are in order to bring about the practical changes we want. By trying to change the outside world to get an inner change (i.e., feel better), we have been putting the cart before the horse.

We spend our lives trying to better our situations, whereas the trick is to improve who we are.

Examine Your Beliefs

First you need to examine your beliefs about who you are. If you like what you are about, then you can hold on to and develop that. If you're unsatisfied with any aspects of who you are, that can be modified just as easily.

Most people merely take themselves for granted, feeling that they're stuck with who they are, that they were simply "born this way." Many people think that life coaching is just about making more profits in your business, losing a few pounds or attracting members of the opposite sex. It can be (and often is) about all this and more, but there would be no point if people weren't happy with themselves after they'd achieved the desired changes.

Change the Way You Think About Yourself

Making changes in your life starts with transforming the way you think about yourself and your life. It's worth keeping in mind that in order for any major positive movement to come about, you have to believe that YOU CAN DO THIS. We are not suggesting that you become a completely unrecognizable person, but rather a person who has earth-moving qualities that transport you to amazing life achievement and possibilities.

You can do this.

TASK

Starting right now you must know more about who you are, or rather who you perceive yourself to be. So first we'll ask you to describe yourself as clearly as possible. Write down the first *seven* major things you think of in the areas of your physical body, your emotional makeup and where you are at intellectually.

This is not necessarily to categorize you, but to find out where you're coming from in order to move forward. Remember, this is not about finding fault with yourself; this is a building process, not a demolition job. Before you begin, take a look at the examples below.

What Type of Person Are You?

Physically—Are You . . . ?

OVERWEIGHT, *toned*, **UNDEMONSTRATIVE**, gesture-happy, **disadvantaged**, advantaged, *slim*, *playful*, PLAIN, *attractive*, STUNNING, *affectionate*, **SPONTANEOUS**, over- or under-sexed, **stylish**, cold, *lethargic*, *energetic*, OBESE, *rhythmic*, BROAD, *unattentive*, **FIT**, vital, **healthy**, ill, *fragile*, *robust*, SMOKING, **stressed**, DRINKING ALCOHOL, *doing the coach-potato thing*, **EATING HIGH-SUGAR OR HIGH-FAT FOOD**, prone to road rage, **slouching**, frowning, *drinking coffee or other poisons*, **not getting enough sleep**, NOT HAVING ENOUGH FUN, *well groomed*, ALWAYS TAKING THE STAIRS RATHER THAN THE ELEVATOR, *having good posture*, **GETTING REGULAR CHECK-UPS**, having

regular massages, **eating fresh fruit and vegetables,** working out, *brushing your teeth regularly,*
participating in team sports, SMILING AND LAUGH-
ING A LOT.

Emotionally—Are You . . . ?

SAD, *joyous,* RESENTFUL, passionate, **optimistic,**
forgiving, *young, understanding,* STABLE, *giddy,*
VOLATILE, *steady,* SECURE, depressed, **pessimistic,**
tearful, *strong, affirming,* MATURE, *flighty,* STIFLED,
delighted, CONNECTED, FUN, aggressive, **"poor me"**
victim, self-righteous, *forthright, vibrant,* GUILTY,
active, DISTANT, *uninvolved,* COMPLIMENTARY, glad,
demanding, independent, *old, codependent,* LACKING
CONFIDENCE, *adventurous,* GLOOMY, *blessed,* **CHAL-
LENGED,** demonstrative, **stimulating,** charged, *capti-
vating, inspired,* BLOCKED, *insulting,* SHINING,
gentle, **giving,** empty, *shy, lonely,* NUMB, *upbeat,*
TRUSTING, *excited,* NERVOUS, insecure, **scared,**
ecstatic, *analytical, living in the past,* FINE, *loving,*
STRESSED, *loved,* SELF-DESTRUCTIVE, worthless,
putting yourself down, off the deep end, *unstoppable,*
sulky, DISTURBED, *balanced,* SERENE, *thrilled,* DEFI-
ANT, animated, **energized,** wound up, *bored, agi-
tated,* CALM, *composed,* TRANQUIL, *relaxed,* ALIVE.

Intellectually—Are You . . . ?

SHARP, *challenged,* SLOW, smart, **argumentative,** confrontational, *stupid, average learner, superintelligent,*
BOASTER, *above average,* INQUIRING, lazy, **daring,**

assuming, *know-it-all*, **focused**, EFFORTLESS, **book-worm**, AIMLESS, *tunnel-visioned*, FLOATY, a leader, **a nerd**, uninvolved, *above average IQ*, **snobbish**, PREACHER, *idiot*, SIMPLE-MINDED, *analytical*, NOT VERY WELL EDUCATED, supercharged, **too old to learn**, challenged, *a follower,* **boring**, TAKE IT AS IT COMES, *teacher,* ACCURATE, *driven,* PLAYFUL, passionate, **consumed**, philosophical, *carefree,* **an expert**, AN AMATEUR, ***an author***, A BULLSHITTER, *dizzy,* DIRECTED, opinionated, **jumpy**, Sparkly, *wise,* **knowledgeable**.

Jot down the words quickly, using the preceding lists to get ideas, without wondering too hard or trying to make it sound right. (If you want to broaden your understanding of yourself in these areas you can repeat the exercise later in more detail.)

Write the positive and negative traits first. Then write what you would like to be, including those aspects of yourself that you would like to hold on to and develop.

EXAMPLE

Excerpt from our client Jennifer's list

I AM . . .

POSITIVE	NEGATIVE	I WOULD PREFER	I WOULD LIKE
energetic	smoker	to be a nonsmoker	vitality
thrilled	codependent	to be assertive	self-reliance, calm
focused	too old to learn	to learn	drive

Scribble away with the first notions that come to mind, as there are no right or wrong answers.

_____

_____

_____

_____

_____

_____

_____

Making the List Work for You

With the positive part of your list, you have identified what you believe your strengths to be. Congratulate yourself on these. Fair play to you! It's important to remind yourself what a great job you're already doing with your life.

Make a decision.

With the negative part of your list, you have identified limiting self-beliefs that have been holding you back. You have also stated what you would prefer to be and to have more of. Now make a decision that you are ready for, and excited about, the next step. Follow the example below, and put your descriptive words into positive statements that follow.

Decision Time

"Decision" literally means cutting off all other possibilities. In other words, there is no going back on this resolution. For example, Jennifer decided that she preferred to be a nonsmoker and have more vitality. Take a look at Jennifer's list below and focus on your own preferences and beliefs, as she has done here.

From now on Jennifer's new self-beliefs are:

I AM A NONSMOKER.	I HAVE MORE VITALITY.
I AM ASSERTIVE AND SELF-RELIANT.	I ENJOY MORE CALM.
I AM A LEARNER.	I HAVE MORE DRIVE.

Making Changes Happen

It's time to move to the next step, which is to believe.

Believe It!

Write your new self-beliefs on pieces of cardstock or other paper, and place these where you can see them—in your car, beside your computer, or on your bathroom mirror or bedside table. Seeing your new identity will remind you constantly of the new and improved person you are. Your task includes affirming these new messages to yourself as often as possible in the tone that is most appealing to you: a sexy voice; a warm, soothing voice; a lullaby voice. Try it out right now— say these new beliefs aloud in an appealing tone. Say them to yourself last thing at night and first thing in the morning, and soon they'll become self-fulfilling prophesies. You won't even have to think about it.

You can also tell your friends and acquaintances that you have made this commitment. Describe the new you to them. This will make it harder to slip back into the old identity. The next step is to act like the new you.

Act It!

The next step is to act the part of the new self. Obviously, a nonsmoker doesn't smoke, so Jennifer now takes deep breaths to help calm her nerves. She drinks water instead of lighting up. She doodles with her pen instead of fiddling with a lighter.

As smoking is a major contributing factor to many fatal diseases, and a serious addiction, people find it beneficial to seek extra help or support to stop smoking. Set out to be more energized or assertive, to take responsibility, and to do whatever it takes to sustain you in your positive self-belief: go to a hypnotherapist, take up mountain climbing, get a buddy system going—absolutely whatever it takes. You know what it takes for you to make it—set a goal to stick to it!

Obviously, this can be the most difficult part for most people, which is why so much of this book is dedicated to techniques specifically related to taking action.

Feel It!

This step relates to your attitude and how you feel about what you're doing. If you are unhappy about your decision, you need to look at the reason behind your dissatisfaction.

- ~ Are you thinking of it as giving something up rather than gaining something?
- ~ Are you feeling less connected to those still engaging in that old behavior?

~ Are you afraid of the change simply because you've been living the old way for so long?

Don't get bogged down with these questions, just briefly examine what might be affecting your resolve and find a new way of looking at it, a way that better supports your decision.

For example, as a nonsmoker:

~ You are gaining health rather than losing a prop.
~ You are finding new ways of engaging with people that don't involve killing yourself, or you are being a wonderful example to family and friends of how they could improve their own lives.
~ You are excited by change as it brings new experiences and exciting possibilities—you're free to walk up the stairs without huffing and puffing, to have that long romantic kiss without the stinking breath and hacking cough, to have the tops of your fingers the same color as the rest of your hand.

A happy nonsmoker can stay off the cigarettes indefinitely. However, it's tiring and uncomfortable to be an unhappy nonsmoker, so you'll be more likely to want to be a "happy smoker" again instead. Martyred nonsmokers are a drain to themselves and those around them.

Your attitude is the making of your overall success. This is where you take a gazillion quantum leaps in one flick of the brain switch. Enjoy your new belief,

Your attitude is the making of your overall success.

smile to yourself, use hand and arm gestures that suggest, "Yes I'm doing it," and give yourself a big high five.

What Do You Value Most in Life?

Often we try to make cosmetic changes in our lives without first working out what it is that really drives us, what we value, what makes life feel "right."

TASK ⟐

Choose and write your top *seven* values:

SUCCESS, *self-confidence*, PRIDE, the physical, **passion**, Vitality, *generosity*, **recognition**, TIME, ***peace of mind***, PEOPLE, *boundaries*, AMBIANCE, genuineness, **caring**, power, *love*, **desire**, EXCITEMENT, ***self-awareness***, CONTRIBUTION, *diversity*, RESPECT, receiving, **youth**, acknowledgment, *honesty*, **growth**, THE PAST, ***the present***, THE FUTURE.

⟐ ⟐

Try to be conscious of how you provide these in your daily life.

TASK ⟐ ⟐ ⟐ ⟐ ⟐ ⟐ ⟐ ⟐ ⟐ ⟐ ⟐ ⟐ ⟐ ⟐ ⟐ ⟐ ⟐ ⟐ ⟐

Consider how you pursue your values, drawing from the list or adding your own. Write down at least five:

_____

_____

CHILDREN, *friends,* **WORK,** holidays, **shopping,** reli-gions, *food, winning,* SEX, *exploring the supernatural,* RADIO, *dreaming,* POSSESSIONS, family, **money,** fame, *fashion, sports,* NATURE, *Internet,* ANIMALS, *marriage,* ADVENTURE, competition, **politics,** television.

Make sure that whatever changes you are making in your life are in sync with your values. Otherwise, you will be constantly in conflict, as your "goals" and your "true self" do battle.

EXAMPLE

If success is your number-one value, and your goal is to spend more time with your kids, you might find it hard to be the new fun-loving parent if it's tearing you away from the work that gives you the much-needed success.

ⓐ ⓐ

Goal Flexibility

Do you see a conflict between your goals and values? If so, this conflict needs to be resolved. Look closely to see if your goals are aiding or working against your values. It's much easier to change your goals than to change your values, and being *flexible* with your goals is the answer here. Can you decide to listen to your kids more attentively when you are with them, rather than just simply putting in time with them? On the other hand, you can redefine success as "having a great family life."

All high achievers have one thing in common. They are completely flexible in looking for better ways to have harmony between who they are and what they are doing.

All high achievers are completely flexible.

Your Life-Wheel

Now let's take a look at where you are on a practical level.

TASK

Divide your activities and interest areas under the following headings. Think about how satisfied or dissatisfied you are with how each is going. Rate yourself between 1 and 10 in terms of satisfaction, 1 being completely dissatisfied and 10 being ecstatically fulfilled.

	1	2	3	4	5	6	7	8	9	10
Money										
Career										
Spirituality										
Creativity										
Relationships										
Home										
Learning & growth										
Health										

Now chart these results on a wheel as shown on the next page.

@ @

For example, if you give yourself 8 for health, 5 for home, 10 for creativity and 2 for career, your wheel will start to look like this:

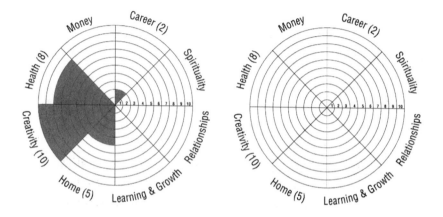

Once you have filled in all areas, you have a strong image of which areas are less developed than others. The optimum goal is to have *all* areas of your life reach their full potential, to have a completely full wheel. How smoothly is your life-wheel currently running? What will you have to change in order to have it grow fuller?

Often people only look at what they are comfortable with and ignore the areas in which they feel less competent, thus making their weaknesses weaker and unbalancing themselves by investing too much time in only one or two areas. Be careful about only playing to your strengths. Often, if you tell yourself that you simply don't value money or love or learning, it's really that you don't feel at all comfortable there.

@ @ @ @ @ @

Be careful about only playing to your strengths.

@ @ @ @ @ @

Further Discovery

TASK ᕙ

Write *five* lines on each, and if possible, share it with someone.

If your obituary was written now, what would it say?

EXAMPLE

_____ was a kind, caring, loving person who will be greatly missed by friends and family.

or

_____ was an outgoing achiever who influenced the community to positive action.

or

_____ never missed an episode of the *Late Late Show* and loved Oreos.

Now write what you would ideally like to have written in your obituary:

_____

_____

_____

_____

_____

Using positive traits only, how would you describe yourself as you are now?

_____

_____

_____

_____

_____

And how would your friends describe you?

_____

_____

_____

_____

What qualities in other people do you really admire?

_____

_____

_____

_____

Are these really your beliefs and values, or have you adopted them from someone else?

_____

_____

_____

_____

What do feel you have learned about yourself from this chapter?

_____

_____

_____

_____

Get together with a friend or group of friends and have fun using the following to initiate discussion. (Alternatively, write your answers in a journal.)

What do you remember your parents or authority figures saying about you when you were a child?

_____

_____

Do you feel this was true of you then?   ○ Yes   ○ No

Is it true of you today?   ○ Yes   ○ No

What is your earliest memory of feeling loved and approved of?

_____

_____

Is it a strong or weak feeling?

_____

How does it affect your current relationships?

_____

What is the one trait that you absolutely could not put up with in a partner?

_____

Is a little bit of that trait in you?   ○ Yes   ○ No

If you could choose to have only one of the following happen in your life, which would it be?

- ○ Earning ten million dollars.
- ○ Your child never getting ill.
- ○ Founding a charity that will help put an end to world starvation.
- ○ Winning an Olympic gold medal.
- ○ Creating a book, piece of music, painting or other work of art that will become a classic one hundred years after your death.
- ○ Finding an island that no one knew about before.

Which of the following would you least like to happen to you?

- ○ Getting taken to court.
- ○ Being imprisoned for life with no parole.
- ○ Losing a limb or your eyesight.
- ○ Going bankrupt.
- ○ Having all your clothes fall off on national television.
- ○ Coming down with a mysterious ailment that means you are always cold or hungry.
- ○ Being hated by everyone you know.
- ○ Being extradited from your country.

What compliment have you received on an ongoing basis throughout your life that has really inspired you?

_____

_____

_____

_____

What insult did you receive that has always affected you?

_____

_____

_____

_____

If someone stole your favorite possession, what's the first emotion you'd experience?

_____

_____

_____

_____

Ten years ago, what did you think your life would be like now?

_____

_____

_____

_____

How close were you in your estimate?

_____

_____

_____

_____

Fantasize Your Future

The Best Possible Life

I n this chapter we want you to shake loose from any old ideas that have been tying you to a certain way of life. Only after you do this can you be sure that the new life you are designing is the ultimate and not just some cut-and-paste, mend-and-make-do project to make your existing life more bearable.

A woman, married with two teenage children, came to us for help one afternoon, feeling quite distressed. She explained that she felt unfulfilled and dissatisfied with her lot in life. After some time discussing how this might be improved, she sighed deeply and said, "I would just love to know what it is that I want in my life."

Many people are searching and striving without knowing what it is they want, which leads to a question: how can you know which life is best for you?

I would just love to know what it is that I want in my life.

The good news is that deep inside you, you already know.

In this chapter we'll show you how to tap into your own personal resources quickly and efficiently, first by getting rid of the psychological clutter that gets in the way of your vision, and then by conjuring up your better life from deep inside you, where it has been resting, waiting for you to activate it.

Only truly developed and courageous people ever do this, as most people don't explore what's going on with themselves day to day, or if they do know that their lives need to change, they remain too afraid to rock the boat.

If you want a new life, you first have to get a clear idea of what you want to get rid of and what you want to get to. In the previous chapter we looked at beliefs about ourselves and what our values are. In this chapter we are letting go of the other deep-rooted, limiting beliefs in order to fantasize freely the possibilities of an amazing future.

"Shoulds"

Often we buy into an idea of what our life "should" be like; we think we "should" follow a certain career path or lifestyle. This mindset (and everyone has one) has overly influenced our choices through the years, often in negative ways.

Perhaps if you've always thought you should be financially independent from family and external debt from the age of eighteen, you might have directed your life in a way that excluded world travel or college.

Maybe if you've always thought you should be married by the same age as your friends, you might have ended up marrying someone unsuitable or currently be stressed about being single or separated.

If you've thought you should never answer back, perhaps you have unwittingly stored up decades of resentment.

The "Shoulds" in Your Life

What "shoulds" have you been buying into in your life? How have you been behaving as a result of each "should"? Here are some examples to get you thinking:

- ~ I should have kids.
- ~ I should be like my siblings.
- ~ I should work at a particular trade.
- ~ I should have more.
- ~ I should have less.
- ~ I should be happy with what I have.
- ~ I should remain loyal to old friends regardless.
- ~ I should be a kind person at all times.
- ~ I should stay in this job because my family relies on me.
- ~ I should only attempt things I know I can definitely achieve.
- ~ I should remember my place.
- ~ I should just be myself.
- ~ I should keep my opinions to myself.
- ~ I should put my kids first.

- ~ I should always listen to my friends' and family's problems.
- ~ I should live near my aging parents.
- ~ I should be up and working before everyone else is awake.

Can you think of any others?

_____

_____

_____

"Shouldn'ts"

Most of us have just as many "shouldn'ts" semiconsciously influencing how we design our lives, such as:

- ~ I shouldn't get ahead myself.
- ~ I shouldn't depend on others for anything.
- ~ I shouldn't think a particular way.
- ~ I shouldn't take the last one of anything.
- ~ I shouldn't step on anyone's toes.
- ~ I shouldn't delegate to get results.
- ~ I shouldn't cry in front of others.
- ~ I shouldn't be overly ambitious.
- ~ I shouldn't talk about my problems.
- ~ I shouldn't try to impress others.
- ~ I shouldn't change.
- ~ I shouldn't mix business with pleasure.
- ~ I shouldn't let my right hand know what my left hand is doing.

~ I shouldn't tell people what I really think of them.

~ I shouldn't be jealous.

~ I shouldn't ask for help.

~ I shouldn't let anyone else get the last word.

~ I shouldn't take unnecessary risks.

~ I shouldn't give others an advantage over me.

Can you think of any others?

_____

_____

_____

_____

MOTHER, *father*, AUNT, uncle, **friends**, priests, *nuns, teachers*, AUTHORS, ***television and radio personalities***

Can you pinpoint where these influences come from? Did your mother or father have "should" or "shouldn't" habits that you picked up?

_____

_____

_____

_____

Other people's "shoulds" and "shouldn'ts" are for other people. A lot of the time, when people get upset it's because they are trying to live by another person's "shoulds" and "shouldn'ts." You're not a kid anymore; it's time to redesign your beliefs and behaviors according to rules that better serve you.

What's Possible?

Most of us also have set ideas about what's possible and impossible, such as:

- ~ Earning twenty thousand dollars a year is possible; earning twenty million dollars is impossible.
- ~ Keeping your kids out of jail is possible; having totally happy and well-adjusted kids is impossible.
- ~ A trip to Hawaii every two years is possible; a trip to China is impossible.
- ~ Having an undemanding, relatively satisfying marriage is possible; having a consistently passionate and outstandingly supportive marriage is impossible.
- ~ Frequently giving is possible; frequently receiving is impossible.
- ~ Learning to say "hello" in Spanish is possible; becoming fluent in the language is impossible.
- ~ A diploma is possible; a doctorate is impossible.
- ~ Quitting smoking is possible; being happy to never smoke again is impossible.
- ~ Thinking young is possible; living young is impossible.
- ~ Dreaming is possible; making dreams come true is impossible.

What do you reckon to be possible and impossible for your life?

Today you are throwing out that old manual and starting as if there are no rules about how life should, shouldn't, can or can't be done. It's time to let rip and dream bigger than ever!

Dreaming

Dreaming is not necessarily about catnapping and discovering the wonders of your unconscious mind. For this stage in your self-exploration, "dreaming" is a form of directing, writing, starring in and watching your *own movie.*

This movie you are about to dream is only about your own future—the most amazing life you could have, the way you would want it if everything in the universe was conspiring to make it true. Make your movie the absolute ultimate. This is not an exercise in dogged realism. If you find yourself dreaming that you're on a yacht, stop that little voice that tells you you'll get seasick. For now we leave all petty concerns and negativity firmly outside in the cinema foyer.

"But," you may say, "I have to think about those family members and employees that I'm responsible for. How can I just run off and star in my own block-buster, kick-ass movie?"

The answer is to dream and desire for yourself first, then you can create ways in which your dream involves everybody else. The fact is, if you're not setting things up so you can be at your absolute best in this world, if you don't connect with your bigger dream, then you won't be doing anyone the highest good.

Or you might be asking "Why don't I dream

something more realistic?" The fact is that the more "realistic" your dream, the more it ties in to your old beliefs and behaviors and the more it sentences you to live in the same old territory. However, if you dream outlandishly, you take yourself outside your comfort zone, and the ultimate results are more likely to be dramatic and dynamic. You wouldn't be working with this book unless you believed that you could achieve much, much more with your life.

Small change is only for the bus.

In his famous speech of 1963, Martin Luther King Jr. didn't have a dream about one day being able to work for a powerful white man, or one day being able to find witty retorts for the racist insults he got on the streets. His dream was that all people would be free and equal, and his life and others were transformed by the power of this dream.

Rather than tacking on ad hoc improvements to your life, we want you to understand that it is possible to design a completely new life without leaving behind people, activities, possessions and whatever else you decide has a special place in the new. It can't be said enough: powerful change needs powerful, big dreams. What makes the members of U2 different from their peers is that, at one time, they dared to dream massive dreams. They dreamed against the current of their times. Bob Geldof saw in his mind how all the famous musicians of the world could come together to compose and perform a song which would feed millions. If perhaps a little voice crept into his ear saying, "But we'd never be able to coordinate everyone's schedules," he pushed that voice firmly aside.

What will you dream today? How firmly will you push aside any destructive little voices?

Remember that everything in life started as a dream. Somebody dreamt of the chair you sit on, the book you're reading, the clothes you wear; someone even once had to dream of you.

Remember that everything in life started as a dream.

TASK

First you must dream yourself a life better than the one you now have (wonderful as that may be), then you can decide to let that dream live or die.

Take some space and time for yourself away from all your pressures. Can you go for a walk, sit by a river or under a tree, go on a retreat, check into a B&B for a night, stay extra long in the shower, relax on a park bench, stroll down the pier, lie in a field, find a quiet corner of the library, sit in a church, go to an art gallery, take an extra hour in bed or in the kitchen, or have the house or office to yourself for a period of time?

My Perfect Life

Sit calmly in your chosen space. Imagine yourself in an empty cinema, sitting halfway up the auditorium. The movie begins with the title *My Perfect Life* flickering large on the screen as music blasts out in surround sound. Allow the images to evolve, transform and clarify as you ask yourself the following questions:

Where Are You?

- ~ Is it a wide-open space or a bustling city?
- ~ Is it opulent or simple?
- ~ Are you by the sea or inland?
- ~ What's the weather like?

_____

_____

_____

Do You See Yourself . . .

- ~ At a party?
- ~ In a meeting at work?
- ~ At home or outdoors?
- ~ On holiday?
- ~ On stage?
- ~ On a particular street?
- ~ At the head of a boardroom?
- ~ On safari?
- ~ On a treasure hunt in a far-off country?
- ~ In an artist's studio?
- ~ In a log cabin?
- ~ At the Olympics—in the stands or on the track?

_____

_____

_____

What Are You Like When You Hear and See Yourself?

~ Laughing?

~ Teaching?

~ Telling?

~ Listening?

~ How energized and healthy are you?

~ Are you tanned or pale?

~ What are you wearing?

_____

_____

_____

What Are You Doing?

~ Are you moving or static?

~ Are you working or relaxing?

~ Are you starting a venture or closing a deal?

~ Are you making love?

~ Are you tending to your children?

~ Are you creating and inventing?

~ Are you receiving an award?

~ Are you helping others?

~ Are you building a corporate empire?

~ Are you writing a huge check?

~ Are you shopping?

~ Are you cooking?

_____

_____

_____

Who Are You With in This Dream?

- ~ Alone?
- ~ A lover?
- ~ Family, friends, colleagues?
- ~ New acquaintances?
- ~ Complete strangers?
- ~ Movie stars?
- ~ Corporate leaders?
- ~ Animals?
- ~ People you went to school with?
- ~ Children?
- ~ People in need of your help?
- ~ Swimmers?
- ~ Movers and shakers?

How Do You Feel in This Dream?

EXHILARATED, *powerful,* CALM, joyous, **loving,** excited, *passionate,* **vital,** DELIRIOUS, *unstoppable,* AMAZED, *worthy,* FREE, successful, **complete,** confident, *motivated,* **driven,** CERTAIN, *in control,* WEALTHY, *blessed,* ACCEPTED, stylish, **awesome,** Wondrous, *magnificent,* **brilliant,** ADORED, *magical,* HONORED, *worthwhile,* REGAL, superb, **glorious,** Wonderful, *outstanding,* **fabulous,** INSPIRED, *first-class,* GORGEOUS, *sexy,* STUNNING, unequalled, **supreme,** untouchable, *invincible,* SAFE.

There can be as many scenes as you want in this movie and as much color, sound and smell as you can possibly pack in. Run it again and again, making it more and more detailed, eye-catching and vivid each time, enhancing the parts that inspire you. There are no holds barred here, no limits as to how fantastic and outrageous you make your dream. Don't be afraid. It really will let you know where your spirit lies.

Once you have your movie running in full color, in perfect focus with all the scenes jam-packed with all your desires, stand up from your cinema seat and walk toward the screen. Now step into the screen, walk over to your dream body and glide into that person. In that body, look all around you and embrace what you see. Now hear what you hear, and feel what you feel. Intensify all those senses, make the colors brighter, make the sounds louder and the feeling stronger. Have a conversation with the person or people with you about how you feel being there with them.

If you find yourself really drawing a blank when it comes to visualizing in this way, relax, take a few deep breaths, close your eyes and allow your mind to wander into your future without any pressure.

Further Aids to Profound Dreaming

Here are some other useful methods for discovering what it is you really want in your life:

- Magazine collage. Take glossy magazines and rip out images that strongly appeal to you. Paste these on a large sheet of cardboard or newspaper. Look to these for inspiration.
- Notice people who seem to be living your dream-life; talk to them if they're available; read their biographies if they're famous.
- Take note of what television programs you find yourself drawn to: gardening, do-it-yourself, political, sports. . . . This will give you big clues as to where your passion lies.
- Try to remember favorite fantasies from books and films that have always ignited your imagination from your childhood onward.

EXAMPLE

One client of ours who craved warmth, security and affection told us that her favorite childhood story was *The Little Match Girl*. When we asked her about it, she explained that when the little match girl lit a match, the tiny flame became for her a roaring Christmas fire with gifts, friends and food around. This was also the client's deepest desire.

What was your favorite childhood story?

_____

_____

One of these, perhaps: *The Tin Soldier, Sleeping Beauty, Jack and the Beanstalk, Snow White, Rumplestiltskin, Beauty and the Beast, Alice in*

Wonderland, Aladdin?

The parts of the stories that most interest you can give vital clues as to what attracts you, such as:

> *Rescuing maidens from dragons*—This might mean you enjoy being the hero or the leader.
>
> *Living in a castle*—This can mean an amazing home is very important to you.
>
> *Surviving alone on a desert island*—This can indicate an ingenuity and independence.

What objects were most precious to you as a child?

_____

_____

What toys and games did you value?

EXAMPLE

A friend of ours who prized her tiny suitcase with her teddy inside now highly values both travel and comforting personal connections.

BUILDING BLOCKS, *books,* HIDE-AND-SEEK, toy cars, **toy animals,** cowboys and Indians, *colored pencils, playing house,* PERFORMING PLAYS AND SONGS, *ballerina dolls,* BABY DOLLS, *soldiers,* GUNS, Legos, **ghost/ witch/nurse's outfits,** drums, *toy telephones, stuffed animals?*

_____

_____

_____

How did you feel about that favorite toy or game? (Only good experiences here, no childhood traumas!)

_____

_____

What do you think it says about the person you are now or the person you'd like to reconnect with?

_____

_____

🌀 🌀 🌀 🌀 🌀 🌀

Realize that in life, as in dreaming, there are no "shoulds" and "shouldn'ts" getting in your way.

🌀 🌀 🌀 🌀 🌀 🌀

Have as many dreams as possible; let it all flow. You know the ultimate dream for you simply because it's the one you return to the most. Realize that in life, as in dreaming, there are no "shoulds" and "shouldn'ts" getting in your way. This new, better world now belongs to you, and you can choose to own it forever and let it live.

Children ask questions all the time and are move alive and connected to their world for doing so. Children are also very sure of their "favorites"—the best friend, the favorite toy—even if that friend or that toy is demoted or forgotten a few minutes later. Thinking of favorites doesn't mean opting for one thing to the detriment of others, it's a way of focusing your thoughts and feelings onto something greater than the mundane or the merely "nice." It's a way of intensifying your relationship to things beyond the stage of liking, a way of escaping the adult tendency to rationalize. If two or three favorites occur, that's fantastic, too. You might want to use the old question, "If you had to rescue one thing from a house fire . . ." By choosing your favorites you more clearly define who you are. Take a moment to write them down.

Your Thought Collage

Favorite photograph? _____

Favorite Christmas gift? _____

Favorite colors? _____

Favorite car? _____

Favorite animal? _____

Favorite TV show? _____

Favorite painting? _____

Favorite old black-and-white movie? _____

Favorite blockbuster? _____

Favorite magazine? _____

Favorite school subject? _____

Favorite physical activity? _____

Favorite creative activity? _____

Favorite idle pastime? _____

Favorite joke? _____

Favorite leaf shape? _____

Favorite expanse of water? _____

Favorite dance? _____

Favorite hero/heroine? _____

Favorite ice cream? _____

Favorite room in the world? _____

Favorite chair for dreaming in? _____

Favorite singer? _____

Favorite music? _____

Favorite actor/actress? _____

Favorite bedtime story? _____

Favorite form of grooming? _____

Favorite movie line to quote? _____

Favorite clothing designer? _____

Favorite cup? _____

Favorite love story? _____

Favorite childhood game? _____

Favorite childhood TV show? _____

Favorite act of bravery? _____

Favorite nightmare? _____

Favorite toy? _____

Favorite childhood memory? _____

Favorite teacher? _____

Favorite sport? _____

Favorite athlete? _____

Favorite precious jewel? _____

Favorite countryside sound? _____

Favorite urban sound? _____

Favorite hunger? _____

Favorite wildflower for bringing home to someone? _____

Favorite garden flower to grow? _____

Favorite sharp smell? _____

Favorite warm smell? _____

Favorite smell to capture a memory? _____

Favorite book? _____

Favorite memory of family? _____

Favorite memory of friends together? _____

Favorite achievement? _____

Favorite texture? _____

Favorite emotion? _____

Favorite handwriting? _____

Favorite house to escape to? _____

Favorite thought to relish? _____

Favorite firm belief? _____

Favorite word? _____

Favorite prayer? _____

Favorite munchie food? _____

Favorite drink to sip? _____

Favorite foreign country? _____

Favorite city? _____

Favorite adventure you've yet to have? _____

Favorite big-time outfit? _____

Favorite fancy costume? _____

Favorite shoes? _____

Favorite season? _____

Favorite compliment? _____

Favorite stimulant? _____

Favorite crush? _____

Favorite outlandish ambition? _____

3

Goal Fixing

Setting Change in Action

There's a way to fix goals in place *if you really want to achieve them,* and that way is not by screaming it at the top of your lungs in a room of drunken revellers on New Year's Eve. How many times do we sigh and whine and say, "I should save money," or, "I should spend more time with my kids," only to have it come to nothing? How many of us have well-intentioned cans of paint sitting out in the shed for that project we never tackled?

It's clear that goal fixing is more than wishing or hoping.

"I wish I had a new car."

"I hope I'll get that promotion."

Have these expressions brought you any nearer to driving that car or having the new executive spot to park it in? Not as they stand.

Goal fixing is more than wishing or hoping.

First, you need to turn those hopes and wishes into goals. It's about deciding that you must make a change and then setting that change in action.

Here's the magic formula.

1. Visualize

Know your specific outcome and really want it. In order to make yourself feel the need for a result more strongly, visualize what will happen if you follow through and what will happen if you don't follow through.

To visualize successfully is to see into your future. Before you go anywhere, you need to know where it is you're going. You don't usually leave the house saying, "OK, I'm going somewhere good." It's more likely that you have some idea whether you're going to the supermarket or to the Bahamas. On some level you have visualized it. So we visualize all the time.

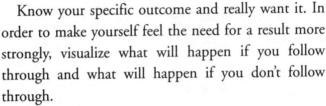

To empower this journey, and ensure we make the trip, we're helped along by this picture. You see the beach, hear the waves, feel the sun on your body and taste the salty air. All of which inspires you to pick up the phone and book those tickets. You will often automatically do the negative visualization as well—seeing yourself sitting around the house for a week with soap operas for comfort if you don't follow through.

It's exactly the same with your other (nonexotic) goals, so why not use this strategy and employ it to your advantage?

Why do you think so many of those Oscar winners look so self-assured? You can bet it's not the first time they're giving that "off the cuff" speech.

TASK ⊚

Sit in a comfortable place with your eyes closed and relax your face, neck and shoulders.

Good Picture

Take a deep breath, and as you exhale, allow your mind to imagine achieving your number-one desire. Picture it in detail:

~ Where are you?
~ What are you doing?
~ Are there others there?
~ What do you look like?
~ What are you wearing?
~ What expression is on your face?
~ What can you see?
~ What can you hear?
~ What can you smell and taste?
~ How good does that make you feel?

Now take that picture and make it bigger, brighter and bolder, and put in surround sound. What an amazing place to be.

If you can have someone read the above list to you slowly as you as you do this, it will help the images flow more freely.

If you can only see the picture faintly and can only connect slightly, let yourself enjoy the visualization again, and keep doing it until it becomes crystal clear, clearer than any film you might see up on a screen.

Bad Picture

Take a deep breath in, and as you breathe out, allow your mind to imagine your life without achieving the goal you have been visualizing:

- ~ Where are you?
- ~ What are you doing?
- ~ Are there others there?
- ~ What do you look like?
- ~ What are you wearing?
- ~ What expression is on your face?
- ~ What can you see?
- ~ What can you hear?
- ~ What can you smell and taste?

Notice how awful this feels. Really engage with the terrifying feeling of not achieving the goal, so that you'll be absolutely determined not to go there again.

Now you really want to achieve that goal, right? Step out of that negative picture and leap straight back into your positive life.

இ இ

2. Be There

State your goals in the present tense. "I am saving money," rather than, "I will save money."

It's not consigned to the future, not something that will happen in an hour, a day or a week, but something already real. It's easier to continue along a path than it is to join one. By stating your goal in the present tense, you are already on that road.

Which of these statements is more likely to end in healthy, baby-pink lungs, and which more likely to end up costing a fortune in duty free and doctors' bills?

"I will give up smoking."

or

"I am now a nonsmoker."

3. Be Precise

The goal is:

"I am losing six pounds by the middle of September," *rather than,*

"I'm on a diet."

Make sure your mind knows *exactly* what the task is.

You say:

"I'm on a diet."

Your brain replies:

"OK, does that mean I can only have chocolate once a week?" (What does your own brain say in this situation?)

Your brain needs direct instructions; it needs a precise end point.

You say:

"I am losing six pounds by the middle of September."

Your brain says:

"OK, I'd better just eat healthy food because that's not very far away. And what else can I do to make this possible?"

Notice how your own brain has a specific plan when provided with a direct instruction. One direct instruction often leads to another, just as one strong command leads to other, equally strong commands.

4. Write

Write your goals up on a big piece of paper.

The action of putting pen to paper is a commitment in itself. If you have to find exact words, this forces you to get clear on what you want. Having it staring back at you creates an objective distance, which means the goal has come out of your internal thought process and into reality.

You can post the written goal up on a bathroom mirror, or somewhere else you can see it every day, where it reminds you, encourages you and holds you accountable. Your goals are now constantly refocused instead of wandering at will around your thoughts and dreams.

TASK ๑ ๑ ๑ ๑ ๑ ๑ ๑ ๑ ๑ ๑ ๑ ๑ ๑ ๑ ๑ ๑ ๑ ๑ ๑

Write up your top *three* goals using the preceding guidelines.

---

5. Commit to the Goal

Making yourself a promise is a form of declaration. People feel comfortable having declared their intentions on an important issue, which is why oaths and vows are such a part of our culture. Once you have a sense of responsibility and loyalty toward something, you are more likely to stick by it. (Ignore the American divorce statistics here!)

TASK

Don't just commit in your mind. Tell yourself aloud, tell a friend, and IMMEDIATELY take one step toward achieving the goal, whether it's throwing out all the butter and cheese or making a phone call.

EXAMPLE

You say:

"I want to earn more money."

You would then take the following steps.

Step 1—Visualize

Good Picture

Visualize yourself paying off a credit card and putting it back in your wallet or a drawer fully paid, or even cutting it up. Imagine yourself using what you might spend the saved money on—the indoor golf course, plasma-screen TV, maid service, home visit from a masseur, the Bee Gees box set—or giving any of these to a loved one. If you decide to invest it for the future, sit down and figure out how much more money it could make from earning compound interest. See yourself sitting on a growing mound of money that starts to lift you high above everyone else. Now see the even bigger things you will be able to experience from that—a car you like, a luxury like a swimming pool, a vacation, an assistant.

Bad Picture

Imagine what the outcome is if you don't save money. See yourself paying interest on the loan, struggling on Christmas Eve to afford that plastic-fantastic ninja-foo-fighter for little Bobby, or rushing to the bank manager to beg for the money to cover unforeseen events such as serious illness or job loss, or arguing with your partner about money, being unable to give the children dance or music lessons, hanging around the house every weekend due to lack of entertainment money—whatever causes you the maximum pain. This is one way to really convince yourself of the vital importance of the money-making goal.

Step 2—Write

Find a piece of good paper and write your goal up in large letters in your best handwriting. Where do you go most often—the cookie jar, the bathroom, your computer, the phone, next door? Wherever it is, choose this as the spot to pin your goal. Hey, go crazy: stick up more than one piece of paper. This will keep the goal in front of your eyes and mind and keep you living it.

Steps 3 and 4—Be There and Be Precise

Write:

"I am making one thousand dollars in overtime in the next eight weeks and having a great time doing it."

Precise (one thousand, eight weeks), positive (rather than, "I'll stop giving the overtime to Johnny.") and in the present ("I am making," rather than, "I will make," or "I am going to make.").

Step 5—Commit to the Goal

What small, immediate steps can you take to achieve that goal? Come up with a mantra, such as, "I can, I must, I am making the money," and repeat it to yourself several times. You can pick up the phone, dial the number and ask to speak to your boss. Talk to your family about the plan to find out if there are any times when overtime would clash with something else important. Put a picture in your jacket pocket of something you are buying with the money. Write a check to yourself for the full amount.

Now return to the life-wheel you drew in chapter one and ensure you have worked out a living goal for each segment.

Check that these goals are in sync with your values so that you won't be in conflict with yourself.

Ask yourself if there are any beliefs you need to change in order to achieve the goals. Does, "I have too many family commitments," need to become, "I have a supportive family?"

Remember
the ultimate
dream.

Now remember the ultimate dream you had in chapter two. Make sure your goals are taking you toward that dream and nowhere else.

The most important thing about a goal is that it starts with a decision that instantly leads to action, which leads to another decision, which instantly leads to more action, which leads . . .

These are the stairs to your dream.

4

Great states

"Great States"— What They Are and How to Attain Them

Can you remember the last time you got into a state of the giggles, when you couldn't stop laughing, or a time you felt very sad? How often have you heard people say, "Look at the state she's in," or "Gosh, I was in a terrible state when I was stuck in the traffic," or "I couldn't think straight, I was in such a state"? Do any of these sound familiar? Everyone experiences different feelings at different times. We refer to this as our emotional states or, simply put, "states."

For instance, if you are going for an interview, you will do your best to be in the best state of mind and body possible. You will act confident and sure of yourself. If you are running in a race or competing in a football or rugby match, you will want to be at your peak performance level. If you are a salesperson, you will want to be clear-thinking, motivated and ultimately self-confident. So "state" can be described as "focused attention" or "a code of conduct."

What state are you in right now? Perhaps you are relaxed, focused and interested. Have you ever heard people say, "When I lose weight, I'll be happy," or, "I know that I will be able to relax when I get home from work," or, "If I could get a date with her I'd be in heaven?" Doesn't it appear that these people rely on situations to create a different and perhaps better "state" of mind? By allowing their environment and circumstances to determine how they feel, they relinquish control over their emotions.

What do you want, and how do you want to feel? By answering this question, you decide what "state" you want to be in. Most people want to feel good all the time because when they do, they become more resourceful, make better decisions and enjoy a greater quality of life. Clearly, everyone's intention, either consciously or subconsciously, is to move away from pain and into pleasure. Now you can learn to change the way you feel by changing your "state," and it all starts with a decision.

Everything We Do in Life Is Based on a Decision

Sure, some things can happen to us that are outside our control, but we decide how we're going to react. We make thousands of decisions every day:

~ We decide how much money to save or spend.
~ We decide whether to drink tea, coffee or water.
~ We decide to take the car or bus.
~ We decide whether to rent or buy.
~ We decide whether to sit at home or go out.
~ We decide to use a blue pen instead of a black pen.
~ We decide what type of person to fall in love with.

Everything starts with a decision—even if it's a decision to do what we have always done. We often think that we are avoiding making decisions, but in fact, that in itself is a decision to *not* take action. Sometimes you think you have passed a decision on to someone else, but in fact, you have made a decision to relinquish control.

"What would you like for dinner?" a friend asks.

"I don't know; why don't you decide?" you reply.

In this case you have just made a decision to have a surprise for dinner. So it's unavoidable—you make decisions all the time. What if you end up being served something you hate, like liver and onions? Obviously you'll make a better decision next time you're asked.

"What would you like for dinner?"

"I would love vegetarian lasagne."

This time you get to eat something you love rather than something that turns your stomach. So, obviously, quality decisions make for better outcomes.

Everything starts with a decision.

Quality decisions make for better outcomes.

Quality Decisions

Ensuring you make great decisions instead of sloppy ones will greatly affect the quality of your life.

What do you regularly decide to do with the money you make? Do you decide to withdraw as much as the bank will allow and leave the remainder in last week's jeans?

A SLIGHTLY BETTER DECISION MIGHT BE:

Decide to stick it in a current account and hope you're not signing kangaroo checks toward the end of the month.

AN EVEN BETTER DECISION MIGHT BE:

Decide to allocate your assets from each check, depositing certain percentages in different accounts to provide for taxes, savings, investments, luxuries and expenses.

You can also change the quality of other people's lives by your decisions. As you dive into your healthier vegetarian lasagne, your friend might see the value of eating better. As you stick to your money system, your children might adopt similar habits that lead to financial freedom. Also, when you insist on being clear about your decision-making process and constantly improve the quality of those decisions, everyone is inspired because they are made aware of the power we all have for changing our lives for the better.

Decision and Action

Included in the concept of "decision" is "action." A decision is not the same as a mere intention. Remember, you can take action to do something or take action to do nothing, but it's all action.

Successful people are renowned for making good decisions quickly on the basis of sound reasoning and then following through (i.e., not unmaking the decision).

We are constantly making, remaking and unmaking decisions, often with very little clarity as to why we are doing so. You might decide to meet up with a friend, and then if it's a rainy day or you don't feel like it, decide not to follow through. You unmade the first decision by making the second. What "state" are you in when you unmake a decision? What specifically are you feeling? What is your body posture like? Are you feeling happy, exhilarated, with your head up, arms outstretched, and jumping or dancing around? Somehow we doubt this very much. You are probably feeling down and in a "poor state"—shoulders down and head tilted or facing down.

Caring About the Results

It's vitally important to be alert to your required result before you commit to a decision. That way you're less likely to play the change-of-mind game.

EXAMPLE

Last year, we were out with friends at a Halloween costume party where everyone looked amazing—really creepy and creative.

For some reason one of our friends, Harry, didn't bother to dress up at all. As we were chatting and drinking glasses of some sketchy green mixture, we teased him mercilessly about his everyday clothes. Several skeletons, vampires and garbage bag witches passed by, and Harry admitted that he wished he'd made the effort, as he now felt so conspicuous he wanted to go home. Even our "supportive" comments about his resembling a zombie anyway couldn't make him feel included.

To start off with, Harry made a bad decision (so did the guy who showed up dressed as a traffic cone, but that's a different story). His first bad decision (to not make the effort) almost led to another bad decision (to leave the party), and if he'd gone home he'd have missed any chance of fun and connection.

Decisions and Mood

So how do you make sure you make fantastic decisions and not end up in a place you don't want to be, feeling things you don't want to feel?

What decisions could Harry have made to have achieved a better result?

Before the party was when Harry could have challenged his "state" by transforming his "poor state" into a "positive and resourceful state." For instance, he could have foreseen the probable outcome of his decision. He could have visualized himself being the only one not in costume. He could have bothered to check it out better. He could have "phoned a friend" to find out if everyone was dressing up.

When Harry made his decision (which was a decision to do nothing and trust to fate), he was in a "careless" state of mind. He cared less than the rest of us about the party and his own good time, or at least he didn't care enough to make a good decision about what he wore. Many bad decisions come from just not caring enough about the process and consequences, not caring enough to relate to the outcome of the decision we're making in that moment. Most smokers, overeaters, procrastinators, career slackers and social hermits fail to foresee, and associate with, the outcome of their decisions. They only think of the immediate short-term effect. This is the blueprint of a poor decision—it only takes into account the "now" or the "soon."

A bad decision isn't made in the moment, it's made in the moments before the moment. Harry had to be in a certain "state" in order to not care enough to find out whether we were dressing up.

TASK ๑

Think of a decision you've made in the past that you wish, in retrospect, you'd made differently. What mood were you in when you made that decision?

๑ ๑

Most people think it's information that affects their decisions, whereas it has been proven that "mood," or mental and emotional "state," is a far greater contributing factor. There's no such thing as "just doing something." We tend to make good decisions when we are in good, positive states, and worse ones when we're in negative states.

It's not your superior dietary information that makes you reach for that cupcake, it's the feeling just before you succumb, the feeling that you "have to."

What feelings do you experience just before reaching for the cigarette, not writing up your resume, choosing to argue with your partner, backing out of a commitment you could easily keep, lazing on the sofa all evening, downing more aspirin instead of going to the doctor, complaining instead of fixing?

Are you in a confident, can-do mood at these points of decision? We suspect not. We suspect that in these moments you're in a specific unhelpful disposition, often just termed a BAD MOOD.

"I Can't Help the Way I Feel"

When talking about emotions, people often say, "But I can't help the way I feel." We have news for you: YES, YOU CAN.

Many people believe that external influences are the only things that can change one's state of mind—things like alcohol, people's comments, prescription or recreational drugs, chocolate, television, radio, particular company, a significant event, gifts, food.

TASK ⑨

What things do you use to make yourself feel different quickly?

_____

_____

_____

_____

⑨ ⑨

If you're feeling bad about having to give a speech (i.e., if you have chosen a bad "state" based on your perceived fear of public speaking), what do you do? Have a drink, push it to the back of your mind, tremble and bite your nails, tell everyone else how bad you feel?

Bad "State" Example

It's really worth examining and dissecting what it is you do and where it comes from.

One day a new client came to us. She was worried that since being laid off six months previously she had been doing poorly at every job interview. She was afraid she'd never get a job again. We asked her to tell us how she had been so successful at doing these bad interviews of late. Her reply was astonishing:

> I just get so nervous my hands start sweating. I start to notice my heart beating, and by the time I get to the interview, my shoulders are up around my ears. I start to say to myself, "What if they hate me? I wish I hadn't worn this suit. I'll forget everything. They'll see right through

me. They'll think I'm a joke." But then I start telling myself the opposite, saying, "I'm OK, I'm OK. I can do this. Don't worry, everything's fine," over and over.

OK, full marks for the positive affirmations at the end, but can you see that this woman was in a really bad "state" for both herself and the interview process? Initially, although she was feeling discouraged, she made an excellent decision to go to the interview and then another great decision to see it through, rather than run away and buy an ice cream.

 However, the moment before she decided to go into the boardroom for the interview, just look what she did to herself! Look at how she sabotaged the opportunity. She believed that the nerves "happened to her," and that afterward things just started to go wrong. Whereas in fact, she unknowingly orchestrated the whole event. How did she do that?

First, she made the DECISION to be nervous. Although it may not have been a conscious decision, she did make the decision. You don't just "get" nervous, as many people think. In order to bring yourself to that state, you have to be focusing on very particular ideas, beliefs, feelings and memories. Some of these are so ingrained that it's hard for us even to be aware of them—we've been playing the old tune so long that our familiarity makes us deaf to it. Some people, like our client, are just very efficient when it comes to getting nervous.

Our client was focusing on the possibility of failure,

the possibility that she wasn't good enough and the fact that her hands were starting to get sweaty. When her hands did start to get sweaty, she took it as "proof" that she was nervous, and so she continued to believe in the reality of her negative state. As she had been running this nervousness program for years, she had built up an identity as a "nervous person," which further reinforced the behavior.

No doubt she was also dehydrated—not something many of us think about. When people get nervous they tend to forget to drink water. Nervousness can then cause them to get even more dehydrated through sweating and expending too much unnecessary energy. This dehydration may lead to a sense of unease, sweatier palms, palpitations and "blurry" thinking.

Our interviewee allowed the tension to build to such an extent that her shoulders crept up around her ears, and this contortion felt so familiar that she didn't put them back down. It's as if she were stepping into a costume of anxiety. As she performed the diva role in her own opera of mild internal tragedy, the lyrics resonated the chosen feelings of inadequacy. "What if they hate me? I wish I hadn't worn this suit. I'll forget everything. They'll see right through me. They'll think I'm a joke." These incantations are based on interpretations of unpleasant memories of perceived past failures. She finally tries to turn it around with a more positive ending to the libretto: "I'm OK, I'm OK. I can do this. Don't worry, everything's fine."

For God's sake, who is she trying to fool?

Despite what she's now saying, every muscle and every thought are completely locked into the conviction that things are disastrous. Due to the fact that she's not skilled at changing from an unhelpful state to a productive state quickly, no well-meaning, last-minute affirmation is going to save the day. She had spiralled down too far to pick herself up and get into a good interview state.

Some people can switch from nerves to confidence in a heartbeat, including the actors, singers and other performers who find themselves throwing up into the fire bucket in the wings and then thirty seconds later playing confidently to thousands. Others can take weeks or months to get themselves out of an unhelpful or debilitating state.

Why not learn to switch at the first sign of nerves (or depression, anger, timidity, aggression, embarrassment, defensiveness, resentment . . .) and save yourself the angst and the poor decisions that ensue?

Good "States"

Positive affir-
mations are
an excellent
way to help
bring about
good "states."

Positive affirmations are an excellent way to help bring about good "states," but are invalidated when our bodies and other thoughts are strongly affirming the opposite. Our client was walking into her interviews in a state of conflict instead of a state of certitude and confidence.

How could she have handled this better?

"I just get so nervous. . ."

Instead, she can decide she is a calm person who doesn't get ruffled in these situations—and begin to act like one. She can identify with times in the past when she was calm, or she can decide to emulate someone she admires who is always collected and coolheaded.

". . . my hands start sweating . . ."

First, she can sip more water and make sure she's not clenching her hands. Instead, she can simply rest them with the palms facing upward for ventilation. She can accept that people's palms sweat a little all of the time and decide that it's a sign of a healthy body and/or excitement that she's going to perform brilliantly. This will stop her from getting nervous about her state, on top of the interview nerves, and so prevent her from making her state worse.

"I start to notice my heart beating . . ."

Great, if your heart's beating, you're alive. Only living people give good interviews, so now would be a good time for her to congratulate herself for meeting this key interview criterion.

Deep breathing is the best way to slow your pulse. It also oxygenates the blood and changes the chemistry in your mind and body. When she decides to focus on inhaling and exhaling from her diaphragm (see "Your Best Health," chapter six, relaxation technique), she'll stop noticing her heart rate, which will start to slow down as the adrenalin lessens due to proper breathing.

". . . and by the time I get to the interview, my shoulders are up around my ears."

This has the result of physically locking in the mental tension, so she can't get rid of it easily. She needs to improve her physiology. In other words, she needs to

Tell yourself
to "fizzy-up."

change her body's posture in order to start to feel better. We like to think of it as "fizzyology"—making sure your body is loose, bubbly and effervescent. Instead of thinking dryly about "changing your physiology," it might be easier to tell yourself to "fizzy up."

"Fizzy Up"

Here's how to do it: shrug your shoulders a few times, then drop them, lower your eyebrows, roll your head around to loosen your neck, look up at the ceiling, smile even if you don't feel like it, stand up and move around like a confident person, shake out your limbs.

All the "tension poses" send messages to your brain to tell you that you're feeling bad, and these messages are reconfirmed by the brain in a vicious cycle. Poor physiology also stimulates the brain to make the body produce stress chemicals such as adrenalin, noradrenalin and cortisol that reinforce uncomfortable feelings. Poor physiology produces more fight-or-flight fuel than the situation requires, which backs up in your body and makes you feel worse than when you started.

"I start to say to myself, 'What if they hate me? I wish I hadn't worn this suit. I'll forget everything. They'll see right through me. They'll think I'm a joke.'"

Would you bring along another person to the interview if you thought they were going to say such destructive and unhelpful things to you? Of course not. So why let yourself be that person? She could have changed the language as soon as it started, saying instead, "I know they'll love me, because . . . ," or, "I'm glad I wore this suit. It's much more appropriate than my birthday suit. I'll remember everything I need to because I've done my research so thoroughly that it's part of me. They'll see what a wonderful person I am with a great personality and will love me as my friends and family do. They'll think I'm brilliant."

Better Results

All these new ways of behaving are a chain of higher-quality decisions that our client had to make to get a better result. When she made them, she found herself more confident in the interviews—she even started to look forward to them. Although she didn't find a job immediately, her interview skills improved dramatically, and she found the job that was truly right for her. She also reported that she decided to use the techniques she had learned in other situations that would otherwise have been a real challenge for her.

When you're in a situation that seems to be heading for an undesirable outcome, ask yourself what decisions you are making in terms of what you are doing with your beliefs, body, thoughts and language. Using this information, how can you make better decisions, and what better places could they lead you to?

TASK @

List *five* bad decisions and *five* good decisions you have made in your past, and write down the emotions you were feeling just before or at the moment you made each decision:

~ Were you angry or distracted before you swore at another driver?

~ Were you giddy before you agreed to that crazy date?

~ Were you calm or nervous before you spoke to your bank manager?

~ Were you happy before you sold that stock?

~ Were you feeling despondent when you aimed the remote control at your TV?

~ Were you excited and confident before you decided to go to Las Vegas instead of your usual vacation home?

~ Were you depressed before you decided not to go out?

~ Were you excited before you quit smoking?

~ Were you self-confident before you lost weight?

In these situations:

~ What was your body like?

~ What language were you using to yourself and to others?

~ What did you believe about the situation?

~ What outcome were you anticipating?
~ Were you successful?

_____

_____

_____

_____

_____

_____

_____

Make a Great Decision Now!

Decide what you are prepared to commit to in order to make better and better decisions across all aspects of your life. These quality decisions will bring you to a higher quality place within yourself and in your surrounding world, and influence the people you choose to keep around you.

Amazing Careers and How to Get There

Doing What You Like and Liking What You Do

Most people are not independently wealthy, which means unless they're going to depend on the government or the goodwill of others, they need to find a way to earn a living. But did you ever wonder why Bill Gates or Donald Trump are so rich but still drag their heads off the pillow every morning to go to work? They obviously get a kick out of what they do and feel a large sense of achievement from it, not to mention power. Many lottery winners keep the same professions they had before the big win, often much to the puzzlement of their coworkers. Some people have careers that result in their being highly paid, while others, such as full-time parents and caregivers, work joyfully for little monetary return.

So it's obvious that work isn't just about the money.

What Does Work Mean to You?

Does work mean a dull nine to five, with the same old sandwich, for eight long hours a day, braving commuter traffic, forty hours a week with (fingers crossed) time-and-a-half overtime for Christmas? Or does it mean excitement, challenge, contribution, great pay and acceptance? Or perhaps all of the above?

When we work, we give of ourselves in return for payment. We usually get paid money, but we can also be paid in recognition, experience, a sense of well-being and a host of other positive rewards. What are you getting paid?

What we give in exchange for these rewards also varies. We can give special skills, physical labor, intellect, personal experience, time, communication, personality and loyalty.

We can also give and receive negative things, moods and attitudes, including disloyalty, laziness, disrespect, awkward hours and so on. If this negativity is ongoing it needs to be factored into the equation when figuring out whether you're receiving enough for what you're giving.

If your boss is constantly sniping at you or undermining you, the big paycheck doesn't seem so sexy anymore. Bullying is a major problem in the workplace. People misunderstand bullying, which can include everything from glaring and snide remarks to full physical and sexual assault, none of which is acceptable. Bullying should be dealt with immediately.

How much happier everyone would be if they could ensure they were completely satisfied with what they give and what they get in the workplace. It's worth remembering that work is supposed to be *fair* exchange.

Is this true in your life?

Work is Supposed to be FAIR exchange.

TASK

Under each heading follow the example below: write out, in some detail, what you are giving and receiving from work in order to help you see if the balance is right for you. Add your own distinctions according to your own situation.

EXAMPLE

What Am I Giving?

Time

I work 8:30 to 5:30, with two fifteen-minute breaks, midmorning and afternoon, and an hour for lunch. Sometimes I can leave early if I have an urgent appointment. Twice a year I have to give up weekends for inventory. I spend one hour a day in traffic on the way to work, two hours on the return journey.

Physical Energy

Little energy is required, except for occasionally lifting sample boxes of merchandise.

Mental Energy

Each day I face new challenges and cope with difficult people. Lots of mental acrobatics are required; I feel mentally drained at the end of the day.

Creativity

I am always coming up with solutions, innovations, plans. I am key player in training days, troubleshooting and brainstorming.

Special Skills

I have a degree in communications, a nighttime diploma in marketing and do ongoing study in computer programming.

Other

My bosses always tell me their problems so often I feel like an amateur psychiatrist.

What Am I Getting?

Money

I'm paid $60,000 per year with three weeks' paid vacation. I get a company pension plan and medical insurance, a $600 Christmas bonus, subsidized lunches, annual profit share, access to a company credit union, and an expense account for training days.

Status

I'm assistant head of my department, well respected within the company.

Enjoyment

I get along well with most of my peers and generally enjoy the day-to-day work. I can read my e-mail and make personal calls throughout the day without being monitored. I like the area in which the office is located, so I look forward to the lunch break and going for a drink after work.

Fulfillment

I'm no longer growing in the job, and I feel very stagnant and physically inactive. In the last three years, I have been overlooked for promotion.

Obviously it's not a straightforward calculation, but would you consider this job to be in good balance in terms of what the employee is giving and receiving? How could he or she make it better?

For example, through soul searching and hard work we have found work we love. Without a doubt our work is often fulfilling in so many ways. The challenges are never-ending as our passion for our work is constantly growing. We get to meet and help exceptional individuals make extraordinary changes in their lives, and we continue to learn so much every single day. From time to time, we have to clear the decks and evaluate the balance. For instance, do we get out for a walk at lunchtime, take a power nap or avoid driving in rush hour traffic, and so on? All of these ideas can enhance our working lives. It is also important to determine what balance means to you, and to know how to achieve it. Someone else's description of balance in their work does not necessarily mean that your sense of balance "should" be the same. It's vitally important to know specifically what balance means to *you* in your work.

Evaluate Your Own Job

In this task, focus on your career and job.

TASK ⊚

Write the answers to the following:

1. Do you consider your own job to be in good balance?

_____

2. How could you make it better?

_____

_____

_____

_____

EXAMPLE 1

If you replied "sometimes" or "never" to question 1, perhaps one of these ideas would make it better:

～ Not eating lunch at your desk.

～ Achieving goals by prioritizing.

EXAMPLE 2

If you replied "yes" to question 1, you still might find the following "time out" idea helpful to improve the balance:

~ Doing stretches or jumping jacks when you have been at the computer for longer than an hour.

People can sometimes find themselves going beyond the call of duty. Do you identify with any of the following examples of giving too much of yourself?

1. Staying late without pay.
2. Listening to people's problems.
3. Compromising your health and safety for the sake of departmental efficiency.
4. Allowing yourself to be yelled at.
5. Doing a superior's job.
6. Continually doing work for which someone else gets the recognition.
7. Putting up with prejudice such as racism and sexism.
8. Compromising family life to meet deadlines.
9. Running errands for others all the time.
10. Compromising your own beliefs to fulfill company policy.

When we go above and beyond the call of duty we can get resentful because we aren't being true to what we are really prepared to give, and often we aren't getting our perceived "just desserts" in return. Out of our fears or our good intentions we can drift into these compromising situations. It's time to identify and annihilate them right now.

Decision to Change

Make the decision to change the situation. If you're not certain about the best way to proceed, seek expert advice. Here are a few methods for taking action:

~ Call a meeting with the personnel involved.
~ Plan in advance what result you want and what you plan to communicate in order to secure that result (see "Troubleshooting," chapter nine, "The All-Purpose Having-the-Conversation Trick").
~ The most important thing is to draw your line in the sand, then don't step over it or let anyone else make you step over it. Firmly set those boundaries, and refuse to be coerced into resetting them in order to appease anyone else. If you decide that you will pick your kids up from piano lessons on time and not allow a work crisis to make you late, then stick to this decision regardless of any pressure you might feel to stay that extra ten minutes at work.

Giving less than you could?

Giving Less

Or perhaps you are giving LESS than you could? This can result in guilt, boredom or lack of self-esteem.

TASK ⊚

Do any of the following sound familiar?

~ Are you leaving early?
~ Doing a sloppy job?
~ Passing your work to someone else?
~ Kicking back and taking it easy?
~ Not taking care with personal grooming?
~ Making company time into social or family time?
~ Making sneaky long-distance phone calls?
~ Using the office photocopier to do your cousin's wedding songsheets without permission?
~ Reading magazines under the desk?
~ Web surfing?
~ Swiping company property?
~ Bad-mouthing the job all the time?
~ Being a grump?
~ Misusing your expense account?
~ Petty embezzling?
~ Lying to avoid confrontation?
~ Calling in sick to go play golf?
~ Showing up for work hungover?

Some of these might seem funny, typical, cheeky or even wise, but are they? This type of behavior might have made you feel proud in the past, or perhaps you were just neutral to it, but it might be worth asking whether it suits the person you really are or would wish to be.

Often people surreptitiously take from the company when they feel they're not getting enough in return. Why not negotiate for better pay and conditions rather than self-medicating with stolen paper clips?

The Right Job

Perhaps you might look at whether you're in the right job at all. Your work has to suit your basic character, simply because you spend so much time doing it that any compromise can have a huge negative effect. It's worth putting in a little effort to find out what job or career would be a fantastic match for your personality type. A first-rate nurse is someone who has, at the core of their being, a desire to help people. A good salesperson is someone who naturally enjoys persuading people, while someone who's genuinely competitive could make a great athlete.

EXAMPLE

Our friend Sally always wanted to make people feel welcome and happy. Even as a child, she got a buzz out of the joy on her friends' faces when she staged tea parties. Later she developed a great talent for home economics, baking and decorating, as this further served her love of giving and pleasing people. Despite some pressure from her parents to go into engineering as her older sister had done, she went to catering college and now runs a party catering firm. Sally made a good choice, picking a career that suited her personality type.

Successful people's skills (unless they are unnaturally coerced and conditioned throughout childhood) will spontaneously stem from their personalities. Sally could have qualified as an engineer, but it might have been against type. Do you know anyone whose occupation is in conflict with their nature? Do they seem happy to you?

It's worth remembering what you wanted to be when you were growing up. You might not think that it's practical to be a princess or an astronaut, but the part of you that needs to be pampered or to strike out into the unknown still lives.

EXAMPLE

A comedian we know comes from a family of eight children, so in order to get attention he became the family and class clown. He later went on to become an accountant, and although he worked at this during the day for years, he drifted onto the stage as a stand-up comedian by night. Eventually he sold his car and gave up the bookkeeping to go full-time as a comedian. He now tops the bill in comedy clubs.

It's all common sense: why become a librarian if you are a natural chatterbox with a short attention span? It can be more subtle than this, too. Perhaps your current job suits parts of your personality, but there might be a profession that would suit your entire character instead.

Successful people's skills will spontaneously stem from their personalities.

Time to Explore

Give yourself some time to explore your strengths and the activities that serve you and really bring out your true nature. After all, you have some amazing qualities that probably only emerge every so often. Can you imagine working and enjoying more and more of who you are, as well as having others benefit from what you do?

It's like this: you can get a job and stay in it because you feel you should, and then end up looking for ways to compensate for what you feel you are missing out on. Or you could fulfill your needs while on the job.

Now is a great time to give yourself the gift of simply exploring the person you are and what it is you need, as well as what you can offer to and get from your ideal job.

Most people whose careers we admire are doing what they love. Bono sings and milks the limelight; Jay Fiedler plays football; Billy Idol sings and gets rebellious; Steve Martin makes people laugh. Our guess is that they're really good at what they do because they feel great doing it.

You might feel that your job is an aspect of your life that's already been decided, or on the other hand, you might be wildly excited about jumping into a new one, but for now, please just play along as if it were all still an open book. The next task is designed to help you change the way you view the job you're already doing, or to make you envision the dream job you've yet to experience.

TASK 🌀

List the following in terms of how important they are to you in a job:

- ~ Intellectual stimulation
- ~ Day-to-day variety
- ~ Creativity
- ~ Sense of belonging (being part of the team)
- ~ Sense of contribution
- ~ Good salary
- ~ Being a good leader
- ~ Being a good supporter
- ~ Opportunity to grow
- ~ Status
- ~ Feeling respected
- ~ Power
- ~ Control
- ~ Independence
- ~ Security
- ~ Mobility
- ~ Feel-good factor
- ~ Great perks
- ~ Easy conditions
- ~ Pension and insurance plans
- ~ Physical comfort
- ~ Good relations

~ Easy commute
~ Childcare facilities
~ Time flexibility
~ Relaxed rules
~ Glamor
~ Promotional prospects
~ Equality
~ Expansion
~ Residual income opportunities
~ Travel
~ Others

If you put security as the number-one thing you value in a job, you're more likely to be happy with a long-term pensionable job with a secure firm than you would be working on a project or freelance basis. On the other hand, if you have independence on the top of your list, freelance projects might be just the thing for you.

Did your high school guidance counselor know you really well? Ours were just guided by our test scores in various subjects. An A in math meant you were steered toward engineering or accounting; an A in French meant you were headed for being a teacher, tour guide or flight attendant; while an A in P.E. didn't count because everyone got one. There may have been some logic to this method, but it didn't take into account the whole person. Perhaps the math whiz might have been happier as an entrepreneur or computer graphics designer. Aptitude is only half the story. Aligning the aptitude, the whole person and the activity—now that's the real goal.

❧ ❧

Be Your Own Guidance Counselor

It's time to become your own best career guidance counsellor. If you've had different jobs in the past, it's important to see these as milestones, or stepping stones, to the job that best serves you and others. They weren't mistakes; they were signs and learning experiences.

TASK ❧

Grab a pen and paper and answer these questions really quickly. Don't think too much about it. Just scribble away with the first things that come to mind. Alternatively, get together with a group of friends and write down each other's answers.

1. What accomplishments, awards and words of recognition do you hold most dear from earlier in your life?
2. What work would you do if you won millions in the lottery? How would you fill your days?
3. What job would you do if you knew that you could never fail?
4. When your friends are telling you about their amazing work experiences and outstanding

personal rewards and perks, how does it make you feel?

5. Write down all the different professions you've ever wanted—is there a pattern?

6. What steps could you take right now that would lead to your dream career?

7. What, or who, do you feel is holding you back?

8. If you were to write an ad for yourself, what would it say? Include skills, experience, and personal qualities and traits. (This is no place for modesty.)

9. If you were to show that ad to someone, how would you feel?

10. Ask your friends and family to think of a career for you. It can be enlightening to note what they come up with.

᭥ ᭥

Using Envy

We are constantly giving ourselves signs about what it is we want. Envy is one emotion that can send great signals. It doesn't have to be a "deadly sin." It's not about hating someone. Really, you're envying the achievement, and this can be used as a motivator, driving you in your true direction. It might not even directly correspond to the job you're envious of. It might be more subtle. For example, if you envy stockbrokers, this might not mean you want to be a stockbroker, rather that you covet the lifestyle or would like to have some sort of fast-paced career in money. If you envy an actor, you might want more attention in your life without having any desire to tread the boards.

TASK ⊚

Below, write down whose career you most envy and why:

_____

_____

_____

_____

_____

_____

_____

_____

People often think that unless they have all the necessary qualifications or background they don't have the right to enter a particular career. If you think about it, most successful people don't have any institutional stamp of approval on their training for the job. Your parents didn't have to gain a parenting diploma before they were let loose to procreate; Oprah was never awarded a master's to be a talk show host. Often, doing (combined with listening and research) is the best training.

⊚ ⊚

If You Think You Might Be in the Wrong Job

Some people feel they have to prove to themselves and others that they have sticking power, that they will see something through regardless of the pain or numbness. Really what they're doing, by staying in the wrong job or career, is prolonging the inevitable and wasting valuable time. Misery does not prove you have great character. Imagine what it would be like to prove you have sticking power in a job you absolutely love.

EXAMPLE

One man who came to us for career advice was miserable in what most would consider a great job, but felt too paralyzed to leave. His one big argument in favor of doing nothing to change the situation was that he had too many responsibilities "dragging him down."

Responsibility

Responsibility can be a joy, not a burden.

However, looked at differently, responsibility can be a joy, not a burden. It means that you have people you're fully connected with in your life. How wonderful it is to know that people trust your ability to provide for them, that you are needed and wanted. This is not just family, as banks and other institutions have trusted you enough to lend you money, and you're a big enough person to take this trust seriously. It's an honor to be trusted. It takes you out of the child world and into the adult world. Being an adult member of society means not just paying the mortgage on time, but taking responsibility for your own happiness. However, some people treat responsibility as a prison sentence, thinking it means you can't move, that you have to be serious and straight-faced about life.

Your loved ones want you to get the most out of life, so don't feel that you are sentenced to a life of drudgery in their name. Instead, know that you are most likely loved and supported enough to take that leap.

Getting a Job

A lot of people make a big deal about applying for interviews and getting a job. There are numerous books on how to ace an interview, how best to present yourself, whether to be outgoing or aloof, and so on. But job hunting is not that scary a process that you need vast amounts of coaching and preparation. The interview is not there to attack you; it's there to allow you to show you are right for the job. Just keep the following in mind:

- ~ Do your research.
- ~ Apply for the job.
- ~ Love the job your going for.
- ~ Communicate the research and the love to your interviewers.
- ~ Look the part.
- ~ Know that the job is yours in advance.
- ~ Be in a "great state" (see "Great States," chapter four).

Training and Retraining

In the current competitive market, special skills and knowledge are your most valuable assets. Sometimes being made redundant, or even being fired, can be a valuable opportunity to reevaluate and retrain (see "Troubleshooting," chapter nine, "Discouraged").

Traditional Full-Time Degrees and Diplomas

In the past there were a great many prerequisites to higher education: the right money, background, class, area of the country, age.

There is ALWAYS a way.

You read in the papers, around college-entrance time, about how difficult it is to get accepted to various programs, but remember, there is ALWAYS a way. You might have to study classics for a year before they'll let you switch to English, but if a department sees you're serious, they will do all they can to get you onto your desired course. Keep focused and you'll get there. Don't stay in the classics department if that isn't where you ideally want to be.

You are in charge of your destiny.

The universities are not in charge of your destiny, YOU ARE, so use what they offer. Many people are intimidated by universities because of how they've been traditionally viewed as the bastion of bookish snobbery. If it helps, think about it as a shop that is selling you knowledge. If you don't know what you want or where to get something in a shop, you just ask. Likewise, call up the nearest university or college and ask, "How do I get to study physiotherapy/architecture/

childcare," or, "How do I go about getting a master's?" Or say, "I don't know what I want to study. Could you send me out a brochure?" Yes, it's not that different from booking a vacation or ordering a bathroom scale.

Before you call, make a list of the questions you want to ask, and if you feel you're getting put off by someone who'd rather be reading the newspaper, simply return to your list and ask the question again, being more specific if possible. If you get someone on the other end of the line who is snotty or unhelpful do not react in an emotional way, stay calm and focus on what you want. Imagine missing out on higher education because of your reaction to someone else's poor communication skills.

The good news is that community colleges frequently have all sorts of affordable degree programs with classes that work around busy schedules and day jobs. Chances are you'd be surprised at what types of options are out there.

Grants and scholarships are also available. They don't usually tell you about these. You have to ask the admissions office—so ask.

Weekend and Night Classes

These days it's not all woodwork, typing and Spanish conversation, although these are still available. You can study law, accounting, dance, broadcasting, self-development and just about anything else you can think of. Ask the office of a community college for their catalog, and you might get some ideas while browsing through. You can also study for many under-graduate and postgraduate degrees at night.

Online and Long-Distance Correspondence Courses

The Internet has developed into a major global source of information. For free, or for a small fee, you can take online courses in investing, alternative therapy and just about anything else. These are usually for your own information rather than for qualification, although some courses will award you a certificate. Increasingly, certified institutions are offering online classes also, especially with correspondence courses.

Long-distance correspondence courses are great for people who, for whatever reason—distance, children, work commitments, and so on—can't get to a college. Some degrees, such as doctorates in hypnosis, are not available in the U.S., so the only way to get a qualification in your chosen field is through a correspondence course.

It's worth bearing in mind that with this form of study you can miss out on the regular study groups and valuable direct feedback you get in other courses.

People Showing You Skills

You don't necessarily need to do a computer course. Get someone to sit with you and show you how easy it is.

Mentoring

If you're hacking through a jungle, doesn't it make more sense to travel in the wake of someone who has just walked before you, clearing the path? Your predecessor might have had to fight off marauding monkeys, had branches lash out to whip him or her across the face, fallen into a quagmire, eaten the berries from the poison jungle tree, and survived to reach the lost temple of the golden light. By observing, listening and evaluating the progress of this intrepid explorer, you can save yourself a great deal of unnecessary jungle fever.

Not only is it essential but it makes common sense to have a mentor. A mentor is someone who does what you want to do and does it exceptionally well. It's someone who inspires you, reinforces what's possible and demonstrates the practical steps to get there.

Mentoring can take lots of different forms. You don't have to be good friends with your mentor; you don't even have to have met them. What's important is that you're emulating their expertise.

Maybe you have felt in the past that there was no one who was an obvious mentor for you, or maybe you've been the stubborn type who believes that something is only of value if you achieve it alone. Not true! You will move faster and more effectively once you identify specifically what you want in your life and find someone who has done or is doing it already. Successful people throughout history have had mentors, even if they have later surpassed what their mentors achieved. In fact, that's the whole point.

TASK

Who could be your mentor now? Scribble down a few names. Could it be:

- ~ A family member?
- ~ Someone at work?
- ~ A lecturer at college?
- ~ An inspiring friend?
- ~ Someone with values you aspire to—
  perhaps a religious leader, a political activist or
  a wonderful person in your community, maybe
  even someone famous?

Who has achieved what you want to achieve, whether in business, relationships, creativity, happiness, finances or any other area?

Once you have identified your mentors, it's time to model them, to do what they have done in order to achieve the required result. Isolate what it is they do or have done that has been effective. For example, if Elvis Presley was your mentor, it would be important to realize that eating fried peanut butter sandwiches didn't get him to the heights of the music industry, rather it was his determination, originality and hours of rehearsal.

The point is NOT to copy *every* aspect of your mentor's life, but to pick and choose those that will result in *your* ultimate success. Having a mentor does not in any way infringe on your originality, rather it acts as a firm guideline that frees you up to be more creative.

For instance, if you want to be superconfident, have an amazing marriage and be chief executive of a company, find someone who has all these things and do what they do. You could find all these in one person, or it might take three separate people. To become as confident as they are:

- Model how they walk into a room.
- Study how they interact with others.
- Note how they look and speak.
- Find out what their belief systems are that allow them to feel confident about life.
- Research what makes their marriage successful. How much time does the couple spend together? How to they relate to each other? What are their beliefs and values regarding love and marriage?
- Trace the career path they took to the top. What type of decisions did they have to make? What type of people did they have to become?
- Learn as many details as possible about how specifically they did what they did.
- This needs to be a complete study rather than just a casual observation.
- If it's someone you know well you can obviously ask a lot of questions, and they can give a lot of advice. It's a wonderful compliment to pay

someone to want to be as great as they are.

~ If it's someone you know slightly, then let that person know you're looking for guidance. Make an appointment and go through specifically what it is you want to learn from him or her.

~ If it's someone to whom you don't have immediate access, someone perhaps like Bill Gates, Anita Roddick or Deepak Chopra, then get your detective hat on. Success leaves clues. Buy their tapes, watch their TV shows, go to their seminars, read their autobiographies and study biographies on them. Don't assume you know how they do what they do—learn it!

Keep at it, and realize that you will probably have several mentors as your life evolves. It makes sense to act discretely and not become a nuisance. Mentors are excellent to "kick start" your career, and it is good to keep in touch with them as you progress. But remember this is *your* life. It is constructive to make the commitment to learn from others, but not to mimic them. Ultimately you have to depend on yourself.

Coaching

Hook up with a life coach as a sounding board and practical guide, and follow through with decisions you make.

Teaching

Teaching becomes the greatest learning. After you learn something, teach it to reinforce the skill. Make it a part of your life.

Life

Fresh experiences, such as travel, working new systems, even mixing in new social groups with people from different backgrounds or age groups, can help you expand. These cannot be underestimated as forms of learning.

If You Are Happy with Your Job

Think of your work as a marriage that might need spicing up every now and then. Here are a few suggestions:

Spice up your job.

- ~ Renegotiate your responsibilities regularly so you don't feel stagnant.
- ~ During the lunch break, discuss something other than business.
- ~ Set personal goals for yourself within the job. What do you want to do? Break the company record for monthly sales, meet all deadlines ahead of time, revolutionize the filing system, be completely open about your methodology?
- ~ Ask yourself what extra value you can add to each project each day. Can you think of something no one else has?
- ~ Become actively involved in the evolving policies and procedures of the company, so you can get a

greater sense of contribution and feeling of belonging.

~ Approach your work with an attitude of fun. Write goals for what emotions you're going to feel, and what emotions you refuse to feel, on a daily basis. "I will feel intrigued about meeting new people; I will not feel stressed when dead-lines are looming."

~ Get creative. If you've been doing the same job in the same way for a long time, is there a differ-ent way you can slant it? Can you change the order in which you carry out your regular duties? If you normally come up with ideas while alone, can you start to brainstorm with others?

~ Are you always just flying in the door with one minute to hang your coat, whine about the traffic and grab a glass of water? Are you famous for being the last into the conference room for a meeting? Start arriving early, and notice the difference that it makes.

~ Stay focused on the job at hand rather than constantly wondering what you'll have for dinner or clock-watching.

~ Remain polite and courteous at all times.

~ Make your work area a more relaxed, energizing, inspirational place to be. Enhance a patchy gray wall with a large framed print of alpine meadows and waterfalls or a grainy photo of a San Francisco jazz club. Put up a Post-it with a posi-tive idea or saying for the day, such as, "Do It

Now," or, "It's Easy." Get seasonal; have a little Santa or pumpkin on display according to the time of year. Display family photos or a potato-print picture given to you by a child.

~ Play soft music in the background if you can.

~ Tidy your desk and the area around it, even applying *feng shui* principles if you agree with them or find them fun.

~ If you prefer the no-frills look, rid your area of any clutter, and find a way to hide all nonessentials.

~ If you're sitting at your computer all day, ensure you have good support from your chair and have good posture so you don't suffer from backaches. Get up every hour and stretch. Breathe some fresh air, even for a few seconds. Drink plenty of water.

~ Really use your imagination when making your workplace "a gazillion times better," whether it's through your communication, the physical environment or the way you organize your work. This applies if you work in a car, a crowded cubicle office, a home office, a kitchen, a palace, a hospital ward or even outdoors doing TV reports or selling door to door.

~ Take note of what gives you outstanding results in terms of improving the working day, and share the insights with your friends and colleagues. Build on what works.

~ The best treat you can give to yourself, and those who work around you, is to watch your mood. Work is not a place to work out your childhood problems or get sympathy. If you find yourself acting irrationally or in a childish manner, maybe this behavior has been triggered by something in your past and has very little to do with the reality of your work situation at the present moment. It's your responsibility to work through this on your own time. No one wants to get yelled at every day because the boss grew up in an angry home, so why should your coworkers have to take the sniveling, sarcasm, lack of confidence, dumping or bullying that results from your own past? Take responsibility and take the necessary action. Join an anger management group, get counseling or just stop the offensive behavior and replace it with behavior more true to your better self.

These same principles apply equally for self-employed people and those who work on a contract basis. Whoever you meet or speak to on the phone on a particular day, you can think of as your coworker.

If You're Happy with Your Job and Would Like Another

If you could do a second job alongside your current job, what would that be? How can you make it possible to include this second string?

EXAMPLE

A client of ours, Paul, had a full-time, demanding job as a regional sales manager. He felt the function of the job was to provide money for himself and his family, and this gave him a great sense of pride. He also enjoyed the work and enjoyed the status of being high up in a prestigious company. For these reasons Paul didn't want to give up the job.

However, at the same time, he wanted to do something for himself, as he felt unfulfilled. He wanted to have more contact with people and see the positive effect he was having on their lives. The indoor, sit-down nature of the job didn't much agree with him either. He contacted us because he'd begun to feel stuck, as if career changes were only for younger people, the redundant or those who had made big mistakes in their career choices. His job was good enough for there to be no real incentive to leave, no pain to escape from.

The solution we worked on with Paul was to become a soccer coach for teenagers at a private secondary school three times a week. As he saw them enjoy themselves, improve their game and win matches, he reconnected with an aspect of his life that had been missing. The fresh air and running around the field probably did him a lot of good, too. He wasn't paid brilliantly for this extra work, but that wasn't his reason for doing it.

He has now also taken on different roles within his original job, choosing to go out and meet people while delegating the indoor duties to office staff.

Although on the surface it might seem that he has less time, in actual fact he creates more time for himself as he feels a lot more invigorated and enthusiastic about himself.

Simple solutions

There are simple solutions to most things. What simple solution can make your work life "a gazillion times better"? Find a way to set that in motion RIGHT NOW. Did you go and do that? If not, please do it right now. We'll still be here when you get back. Great. Life is lighter when you're doing what makes you feel true to yourself.

You must be passionate about what you do.

It all boils down to this: you must be passionate about what you do. If you're doing something you love, then you'll never work a day in your life.

How to Survive Office Politics

Don't join in the negative stuff

One Big Rule: DON'T JOIN IN THE NEGATIVE STUFF.

If you're not in the right career for you—fully stretched, unstressed, fulfilled and excited—then you're going to indulge in practices that don't serve your best self. If you find yourself identifying with any of the following characters, now is time to look at why you're doing what you're doing, and stop and do something different instead. Often people can feel bad about being negative all the time and feel there's something wrong with them, whereas in fact, there is only something wrong with what they're doing. It's time to wise up and take a long, hard look at the way you've been acting.

The Kit-Kat Chatterbox

These people are pretty harmless, or so they believe. But idle gossip, even when not fully believed, can sour a community. When everybody's sitting around involved in the chat of the coffee break, they want to feel as if they belong. If gossip is the easiest, most sure way they know of getting a reaction and connection, this is what they'll do. Notice that gossiping has a different tone than when we talk about ourselves or those in the room. It sounds conspiratorial, dramatic, holier-than-thou.

Why not be the "constructive center" of the coffee break instead? This doesn't mean being a goody two-shoes, because finding the positive can be every bit as bonding and entertaining as gossiping used to be.

✐ ✐ ✐ ✐ ✐ ✐
Find the positive.
✐ ✐ ✐ ✐ ✐

The Underhander

These people are lovely to everyone on the surface and are the whole world's friends. They can make you feel needed and special. But their fears about their own abilities, or job security, cause them to be completely disloyal and make unnecessarily negative reports about people in a "professional capacity." For example, if they fear they won't get a particular promotion, instead of going on a weekend seminar to get better qualified or taking on more responsibility, they'll underhandedly start rumors about the other job candidates. They might exaggerate someone's drinking habit in a concerned tone ("I'm really worried about Steve"), or jovially mention that a woman might be looking to get

✐ ✐ ✐ ✐ ✐ ✐
Be real and genuine.
✐ ✐ ✐ ✐ ✐

pregnant and leave work ("Isn't that great for her?") or laugh about how it's ". . . hilarious the way Anna can't do simple accounts."

Why not be real and genuine? Usually people in fear are worried that being genuine "won't work." No job pays enough that it should rob you of your best.

The Office Brown-Noser

These are the people who suck up to those in command. Their behavior would sometimes lead you to believe there was a film star on the premises, as they fetch drinks, stay late and ensure the object of their attentions knows all about it. Think Smithers sucking up to Mr. Burns in *The Simpsons,* but without the love overtones. They believe that excessive personal adoration is the best way to move up through the ranks. Often, however, bosses are fatigued by this constant attention and can see right through it. They begin to doubt the integrity of the individual and wonder if those who play lacky have any real belief in their abilities.

Life is very tiring for office brown-nosers because their sense of well-being often relies on the reaction of one person. Instead, these people could develop more respect for themselves and concentrate on their jobs rather than the boss.

Concentrate on the job

If you are a boss, you might want to evaluate whether you are rewarding this type of fawning behavior or rewarding a job well done. The latter will obviously lead to a healthier company.

The Flirt

This man or woman can't leave the nightclub in the nightclub. Harmless flirting is natural, fun and can lead to a more relaxed work atmosphere. But the context is all-important here. Flashing a smile and a witty retort is one thing, but power flirting, as if the office were the only place to find a mate, is another thing entirely. Excessive flirts are often just in need of attention and affirmation, and might want to find better ways of achieving these goals. Notice if your behavior is making anyone uncomfortable and adjust your actions accordingly. Be warned that you can be perceived as being unfocused and not worth taking seriously. There is also quite a thin line between flirtation and sexual harassment, so check that you're on the happy side of that line.

Be a "friendly flirt" not a "powerhouse puller."

Be a "friendly flirt" not a "powerhouse puller."

The "Love Me, Love Me" Person

These people-pleasers will fall over themselves doing whatever it takes to make everyone happy, to the extent that their own work often suffers. They'll be the one to buy the fanciest pastries for the coffee break; they'll drop anything to listen to your problems; they'll offer to take care of everyone's cats and dogs when they're on vacation—sometimes to the point of seeming intrusive. The difference between a regular nice person and a "love me, love me" person is that the latter has great difficulty saying no to any request and will go overboard in the effort to make everyone happy. Although they might come across as a little ray of sunshine, they are usually not strong and grounded within themselves. This leads them to overcompensate with pleasing actions, as they think they need other people's recognition and gratitude to make them feel whole.

If you are, or associate with, this character type, it's time to set some boundaries. Ensure that your primary recipient for good attention is yourself. Choose wisely who you give to, and ensure that you are also receiving. Giving until you are empty serves no one. Besides, you are being paid to do a certain job, and it's worth making sure this is not suffering. No single person is solely responsible for creating a pleasant atmosphere in the workplace.

Giving until you are empty serves no one.

Your Best Health

Maximize Your Energy, Health and Vitality

There are hundreds of thousands of books, tapes and seminars advising the world as to the best way to take care of our bodies. Some say jogging is good for you; some say jogging is bad for you; some say to avoid proteins; others say to avoid carbohydrates. So what are we to believe? And what are we to do?

As no two bodies in the world are alike, individuals will find some aspects of this chapter more useful than others. Some of you reading this might believe you are beyond hope, while some of you have been taking such good care of your bodies that you wonder what this section has to offer you. If you're tempted to skip this chapter, please read it through to the end, as we believe there are always new things to learn and ways to improve. After all, you've come this far in making massive improvements in your life. You deserve a fantastic, healthier body, too.

We are not about to make you feel bad for having a chocolate fetish, for staying up late or for not sweating it out at the gym five times a week. But we do want you to get out of the armchair and leap into your life with a sense of passion, certainty and happiness. We won't take away your bag of potato chips, but we do warn you that in a few pages time, you might throw it away of your own volition. It's not an all-or-nothing scenario—where you're either a couch potato or an Olympic athlete, a five-burgers-a-day man or a vegan—it's about what works for you.

Over the next few pages, we will be exploring how you can best take care of your body in order to have the maximum possible energy, health and vitality.

The healthier you feel, the more dramatically all other aspects of your life will radiate with constant energy. Some people wage an ongoing battle with their bodies—an attitude that doesn't lead to the effortless way of being they wish to attain.

Asthma, heart disease, cancer, stress, obesity, lethargy, arthritis, depression, chronic fatigue syndrome and other illnesses are so prevalent in society today that many have come to believe these are a natural part of life. However, many illnesses and diseases are caused by poor lifestyle choices.

Pollution, cigarette smoking, overeating, reduced

physical movement, negative thinking, poor nutrition and lack of exciting prospects are tragically so much a part of so many people's lives that a full sense of well-being is something they have yet to enjoy.

Rather than trotting off to your doctor and pharmacist to combat those sniffles and sneezes and aches and pains, why not save yourself time, money and discomfort? Why not cure yourself ahead of time by preventing disease in the first place? You've heard it before—prevention is the best cure—but there's no point in having the information unless you put it into play.

Prevention is the best cure.

No matter what your age or current health and fitness levels, the body has a remarkable ability to heal itself. It's true that many diseases have genetic causes, but this doesn't mean that coming down with the disease is inevitable. In these cases, it's even more important to take care of your body, so as to avoid triggering the genetic predisposition.

The first step to any improvement is to take note of where you are at right now.

It's Time to Strip Naked!

Take all your clothes off and stand in front of the mirror (if you are reading this during lunch break at work or on the train please wait until you get home!). Remove every stitch, and leave the lights on. If you are like most people, you might instantly start to criticize what you see. Your first task is to look at your body uncritically and take stock:

~ Look at your legs, and think of all the support
   they have given to you and all the places they
   have taken you so far.
~ Look at your stomach and think of all the
   wonderful meals it has digested for you.
~ Look at your chest and reflect on how it has
   protected your beating heart through good and
   bad times.
~ Look at your arms and remember all the people
   they have held close and the burdens they have
   lifted.
~ Look at your head and be fascinated at the great
   job it has been doing protecting your brain.
~ Gaze into your eyes and marvel at the memory
   of all the incredible sights you've witnessed since
   you were born.

You see, it's easy to be friends with your body when
you remember all the fantastic ways in which it serves
you. This is just the tip of the iceberg. Inside you there
are billions of fascinating mechanisms working in harmony to ensure that your body functions as it was
designed to.

Now let's consider how you would like to have fun
improving that invaluable body. Here are some suggestions for how to thank your body for all it has done
for you:

~ Swap the beer belly for a different kind of
   six-pack.

*Have fun
improving
that invalu-
able body.*

~ Build those bird legs into gladiator limbs, or turn tree trunks back into saplings.

~ Cut the junk food down to once a week or less.

~ Lose the stoop and stand tall.

~ Finish reading this chapter.

~ Get together with a friend who will join you in your health drive.

~ Pump the pecs and biceps.

Make your decisions based on what you want to achieve for your body, rather than being fueled by insecurities based on comparisons with other people's bodies. Take the goals you have had for your body that you have been struggling with and either:

a) Recommit to those goals and find a better way to get there or,

b) Set aside the original goal for now and concentrate on achieving a completely new goal.

If you have been trying to lose six pounds, either change the way you've been eating for weight loss, or decide for now to trim and tone your muscles.

Eat Healthy

Eating is obviously a vital component of health, as we have to eat to live.

TASK   @

Answer the following questions about your concept of healthful eating, based on your regular day-to day life.

1. What's a healthful meal for you?
   - Having a fried tomato along with your steak and fries?
   - Grilling your steak and having a baked potato and stir-fried vegetables?
   - Having some grilled fish with steamed vegetables?
   - Snacking on a handful of crackers with cheese?

2. What is your relationship with food? Is food:
   - ~ Your enemy?
   - ~ Your friend?
   - ~ Your savior?
   - ~ An inconvenience?
   - ~ An expense?
   - ~ A celebration?
   - ~ A comfort?
   - ~ A necessity?
   - ~ An adventure?
   - ~ A fix?
   - ~ A great way to fill the time between *Survivor* and *American Idol*?
   - ~ A sharing opportunity?
   - ~ Energy?

~ A punishment?

~ Just there?

3. Do you feel this attitude toward food makes you more or less healthy? Is there another attitude you can adopt that will make you happier to be healthy in the long run? How many meals do you have in a day? Two, three, four or more, or just one that lasts all day?

List everything you have eaten in the last forty-eight hours. Include the times at which you ate and what happened before and after eating. What did you discover? Did you eat more or less when you were angry, tired or stressed? Did it affect the type of food you went for?

4. How do you eat? (And we don't mean with your mouth opened or closed, or with your fingers or toes.)

~ Do you eat quickly or slowly?

~ Do you chew well or wolf it down?

~ Are you uptight or relaxed when you eat?

~ Do you eat with people you like or dislike?

~ Do you enjoy eating alone or with others?

~ Do you eat on the go or sitting down?

~ Are you always in front of the computer or TV as you eat?

~ Do you eat after getting home late at night?

5. What is your best memory of an eating experience? What was particularly enjoyable about it? Notice where you were, who you were with, and what you were eating.

It's a good idea to know something about the habits you are wanting to improve upon, because we can't change our habits unless we identify what it is we're changing. You want to change the cause rather than just the symptom.

If you have a pastry every day at eleven o'clock, and this is a ritual you always share with your mother, then you might want to find another ritual to share with her rather than just giving up the pastry "cold turkey."

If you find yourself binging after an argument, then maybe you need to examine the feelings you experience in that situation—perhaps rejection, hurt, anger, dissociation. It's wanting to fix those feelings with food that can cause people to binge.

Everyone has different eating habits. It's up to you to decide on your rate of change into a more healthful eating pattern. Gradual change can ensure an easy transition into healthful eating, and rapid change can empower you more quickly. Swap the fries for a baked potato first, and have one spoonful of vegetables if you don't normally eat any. If you fry foods, start to grill and steam them instead. Stop having an appetizer and dessert with every dinner. Even the smallest of changes can make a huge difference.

Even the smallest of changes can make a huge difference.

There are three main emotional contributory factors associated with overeating: stress, depression and nervous anxiety. Ask yourself whether any of these are related to your current eating habits.

What Is Healthful Food?

Healthful food is what works for your body and makes you feel good. For example, if you eat a meal and a few minutes later you feel tired, hungry, restless or irritable, this is typically due to the fact that something you ate does not suit your body. If a particular food doesn't agree with you, then cut it out. Another general rule of thumb is to eat freshly grown foods rather than processed foods. Fresh foods retain most of their goodness, have little or no additives or preservatives, and contain nutrients that the body can efficiently use.

Diets are pastimes not solutions, so don't get faddy. If you want to get healthy, change your eating style for life.

Shopping

The big make-or-break moment is when you hit the supermarket or late-night corner shop. Before setting out to shop, make sure you've eaten a nourishing meal, otherwise you'll be piling all the high-calorie foods into the basket as your craving dictates to your brain. Make a list before you go, and stick to it. Work out in advance what fresh foods you are likely to need that week. Take into account whether you are scheduled to dine out a lot, how many people will be in the house and how much time you'll have for food preparation.

Get label-wise. Just because a product says "90 percent fat free" on the box does not make it a healthful

If you want to get healthy, change your eating style for life.

food or low in calories. Get familiar with the percentages of salt, fat and sugar contained in the foods you buy. These days most vegetarian products are marked. There are many healthful alternative foods available, so read and compare labels and familiarize yourself with what's going into your body. Fresh fruit, vegetables, nuts and grains are always the best option.

Get label-wise.

Eating Out

Eating out at social events is often an excuse for people to eat less-healthful foods. In a restaurant, go for the leaner menu choices such as grilled fish, chicken, salad and tomato-based sauces. The chef can often modify a dish for you to suit your nutritional needs. In the past many people found it difficult to be assertive in public situations, but these days you can be proud to ask for what you need and assure you get it.

Enjoy the food, but don't feel you have to finish everything on your plate. Stop when you're almost full. Going overboard on the bread basket and the butter can often be a result of nervousness or boredom before the main course arrives, so decide in advance what you are going to do instead of nibbling on a roll.

Eating out is a social event, not a gorging event, so keep your focus on being with people and enjoying their company. Really taste the food, and know that you are enjoying it. If you feel that you tend to overeat at a restaurant or party, preempt the situation and wear something a little tight around the waist as a reminder. Put down your knife and fork between mouthfuls, chew slowly, engage in conversation and keep sipping water.

Eating at Home

The biggest reported problem for people trying to eat healthy in families is that they feel they have to eat the same as everybody else. They claim they can't prepare a separate meal for themselves, but often this has more to do with not wanting to single themselves out or be the focus of negative attention. Many a teenager giving up meat has been subjected to comments such as: "You need meat for strength;" "I'm so worried you won't get enough vitamins and iron;" "I suppose your friends have just turned vegetarian;" "You're only cold because you don't eat meat any more."

Explain to your family in advance why you're making the changes. Bear in mind you can modify the meal that the whole family eats, giving yourself more vegetables and substituting more healthful options, such as chicken, tofu, kidney beans, veggie burgers or fish.

Many people work at home, and for them the temptation is to graze throughout the day—often as an excuse to get away from the work station. It's very important for these people to set themselves definite mealtimes and productive activities for their breaks.

Portion Sizes

Look at your portion sizes. Your stomach is only the size of your fist, so make a power fist as you go into the kitchen or restaurant just to remind yourself of this. Are you piling your plate too high? What size plate are you using? Is it too big or too small? If you eat processed foods, again, read the packaging, and see whether you are eating a meal alone that is intended to serve two or three people.

Working Out

What is working out? Working out can mean walking around the garden or the block; it can mean carrying the shopping bags in order to tone the muscles rather than putting everything into the trunk of the car; it can mean

DANCING AROUND THE KITCHEN TO YOUR FAVORITE POP SONG, *jumping on a mini-trampoline,* CLIMBING A TREE, lifting your kids up and down, **rollerblading,** skiing, *gardening, ballroom dancing,* SALSA DANCING, *stretching, yoga,* T'AI CHI, *martial arts,* FOOTBALL, hockey, **ice skating,** belly dancing, *running, putting more energy into the housework,* WALKING THE DOG, *polishing the silverware,* HORSEBACK RIDING, *mowing the lawn,* CYCLING, sailing, **kickboxing,** Scuba diving, *great sex, polo,* BOWLING, *tap dancing,* GOLFING, *aerobics,* SKIPPING, aqua-aerobics, **weightlifting,** doing cartwheels and handstands in the yard, *hula hooping, swimming with dolphins.*

Successful workouts are all about having the mindset to move your body energetically and with passion on a consistent basis. It's not something you have to do, but something you automatically do, something that is an effortless part of your lifestyle. Let's vow to never again utter the phrase, "I really should go to the gym." Only go to the gym if you love it passionately.

However, you can trick yourself into being more excited about exercising:

- ~ Tell yourself you'll just go to the jacuzzi or sauna, but once you're there you're likely to feel more compelled to involve yourself in other activities offered at the health club.
- ~ Just walk to the corner of the street, and the momentum is likely to build, causing you to walk around the block or farther.

You can trick your-self into being more excited about exercising.

Moving your body needs to be something you do to feel good, not something you do in order to prevent yourself from feeling guilty. When you exercise, chemicals called endorphins are released from the brain into the bloodstream. These are the happy chemicals that make you feel fantastic.

In order to keep up a good exercise routine, it is essential to eat healthfully on a regular basis to ensure you maintain enough energy for the activity.

If you're taking up a new, vigorous form of exercise, it's important to notify your doctor and obtain instruction from a competent professional coach or trainer.

Take Care of Your Body

There are so many other ways to take care of your body. These days there are a vast number of alternative and complementary treatments and therapies available. Some might find acupuncture helpful to ease tension headaches, while others might find a head, neck and shoulder massage equally effective. These are areas you can research in a practical way to find out what is best for you.

Check out the following:

Acupuncture

Acupuncture is an ancient Chinese system of healing. This system, which has been widely used in the West for over thirty years, involves the use of fine needles at specific points in the body to achieve various therapeutic effects. The aim of acupuncture is to determine the underlying causes of disharmony in the body and to rectify them with the use of needles.

Alexander Technique

The Alexander technique was developed by F. M. Alexander in the nineteenth century. This technique is about becoming more aware of the way your body works, particularly the bones and muscles that are designed to sit. It's about realigning the body to get rid of unwanted tension and old habits that cause unnecessary wear and tear.

Aromatherapy

Aromatherapy transforms through the sense of smell. It involves the use of essential oils, which can reduce negative moods and generally help balance emotional states. Diluted essential oils can be used for massage and in the bath to soothe or revitalize the body.

Chiropractic

Chiropractors readjust the skeletal structure, in particular the spinal column, to enable it to better perform its function. Slight displacement of the spine can cause pressure on nerves, which can negatively affect other parts of the body. Adjustment techniques include physical manipulation of affected joints, and usually a course of treatments is required. It is highly effective for the relief of back pain and aching joints.

Colonic Irrigation

Colonic irrigation is a process in which the colon and lower intestine are washed out with water and other liquids. The purpose is to rid the body of old, compacted and solidified feces.

Counselling

Counselling can be highly beneficial for people who feel the need to discuss and release current troubles or past traumas. This can only work effectively when there is a specific goal in mind, such as feeling better and leaving the past in the past. It's important to remember that health includes body and mind.

Emotional Freedom Therapy (EFT)

By tapping on specific meridians (pressure points on the body), EFT can be used as an effective therapy for trauma, stress, depression and addictions, to name but a few. Although still in the experimental stage, it often works when nothing else seems effective. The treatment is pain-free, rapid and can be self-administered.

Homeopathy

Homeopathy was introduced by German physician Samuel Hahnemann in the eighteenth century. Homeopathic remedies are found in plants and animals, naturally occurring rather than processed. The treatments, which can be adjusted to suit each person, are thought to act by stimulating the immune system.

Hydrotherapy

Hydrotherapy is the use of water for healing purposes. Treatments can include high-pressure hosing with hot or cold water, body wraps, Turkish baths, foot baths, whirlpools, etc. Benefits include reduced blood pressure, increased lymphatic drainage, stress relief and improved circulation, and so on.

Hypnotherapy

Hypnosis can be described as an altered state of awareness or a deep state of relaxation. The trance state is similar to meditation. The hypnotherapy process bypasses the critical faculties (conscious mind),

communicating suggestions directly to the unconscious mind. Hypnotherapy is widely used to help create behavioral change and is highly effective in pain
control.

Makko Ho

Makko Ho is an Eastern approach to relaxation
with reference to the five Chinese elements of earth,
water, fire, wood and metal. It's based on awareness of
your breathing and observing the body and how it
responds to your emotions. Makko ho exercises are
practiced once a day to enhance the natural flow of
energy within the body.

Massage

Massage is recognized as an ancient form of healing.
The manipulation of muscle tissue relieves stress, eases
aches and pains, and improves circulation.

Meditation

Meditation is a philosophy of peacefully reflecting
on how you are instead of who you are. By meditating
at least twice a day for twenty minutes or so, you can not
only feel rejuvenated and relaxed but also connected to
your resources and inner strength. It is widely used to
combat stress and bring relief to people suffering from
serious illness.

Neuro Linguistic Programming (NLP)

Neuro linguistic programming was developed by Dr. Richard Bandler and Dr. John Grinder in the late 1970s. It's a breakthrough science of personal behavior. "Neuro" stands for the brain, "linguistic" refers to the language we use, and "programming" is our learned behavior or conditioning. NLP has been described as the user's manual for the brain and is used to bring about behavioral changes from within.

Osteopathy

Osteopathy was founded by Dr. Andrew Taylor Still in 1874. It is based on the philosophy that although we stand upright, our bodies still feel as though we were on "all fours," as our predecessors were. Similar in many ways to chiropractic therapy, this technique involves treating the whole body, not simply the spine.

Reflexology

Reflexology is based on pressure points in the feet and other parts of the body which correspond to internal organs. Thus pressure or massage on these areas can stimulate improved organ function.

Reiki

This is a gentle hands-on treatment that stimulates the flow of the energies around the body. It's recommended for maintaining emotional health and is specifically useful for people who have been through physical and emotional trauma, as it realigns the positive energies.

Shiatsu

Shiatsu has been described as Japanese physiotherapy. Similar to acupuncture, the technique involves energy lines (meridians) and pressure points. The practitioner applies pressure to the person's body using thumbs, fingers, elbows, hands and knees.

Health is ultimately about maintaining a balance in the body and mind. Remember the basics:

- ～ Ensure that you eat healthfully.
- ～ Get plenty of fun exercise.
- ～ Drink loads of water.

Just as important is making sure that you have time for relaxation. Be vigilant with regard to what causes you stress so that you don't go beyond your limitations.

Laugh and smile as much as possible.

Relaxation Technique

This simple procedure can be done for between three and twenty minutes whenever you can safely switch off the outside world.

- Get comfortable in a seated or lying position.
- Squeeze your facial muscles as tightly as you can, count to three and relax again. Do this three times.
- Make tight fists with your hands to the count of three, then release the tightness. Do this three times.
- Squeeze your toes as tightly as you can to the count to three, then release tension and relax. Do this three times.
- Focus on your breathing as you inhale deeply. Breathe in, and hold each breath for the count of three. Then exhale, and count three again. Repeat this three times.
- Continue breathing easily and freely.
- Repeat a sentence or word that is especially pleasing to you, such as, "Gently relaxing," "Feeling at ease," "All is safe in my world," or "Relax now." Do this a few times until you are calm and clear-headed.

Try Eating Something New Today

Breakfast

Chop up an apple, an orange, half a banana and a pear. You can leave the skin on the apple and pear if this suits your taste. Put them into a bowl and pour a small tub of soy yogurt over the chopped fruit. Pour a small spoonful of honey over this and finish off with a sprinkling of wheat germ or crushed nuts.

Lunch

Slit open a pocket of brown pita bread, and heat it in a oven. Chop up two leaves of your favorite type of lettuce, a spring onion, a tomato and half a roasted bell pepper or a small spoonful of sweet corn. Mix in some chopped tuna, chicken or smoked tofu with dressing or pickles to taste. Fill the toasted pita pocket with the mixture.

Dinner

Chop up a small bowlful of your favorite vegetables and stir fry them in half a tablespoon of olive oil with some mixed herbs to taste. Cut a large red bell pepper in half and scoop out all the seed and white bits.

Now take the vegetable mixture and stir in a cup of breadcrumbs and a dash of lemon juice. Fill the two pepper halves with the mixture and place on a lightly greased baking tray. Bake in a moderate oven for forty minutes, or until the pepper cases are soft and mottled brown.

ENJOY!

READER/CUSTOMER CARE SURVEY

We care about your opinions! Please take a moment to fill out our online Reader Survey at **http://survey.hcibooks.com**. As a **"THANK YOU"** you will receive a **VALUABLE INSTANT COUPON** towards future book purchases as well as a **SPECIAL GIFT** available only online! Or, you may mail this card back to us and we will send you a copy of our exciting catalog with your valuable coupon inside.

(PLEASE PRINT IN ALL CAPS)

First Name _____ MI. _____ Last Name _____

Address _____

State _____ Zip _____ City _____ Email _____

1. Gender
- ☐ Female
- ☐ Male

2. Age
- ☐ 8 or younger
- ☐ 9-12
- ☐ 13-16
- ☐ 17-20
- ☐ 21-30
- ☐ 31+

3. Did you receive this book as a gift?
- ☐ Yes
- ☐ No

4. Annual Household Income
- ☐ under $25,000
- ☐ $25,000 - $34,999
- ☐ $35,000 - $49,999
- ☐ $50,000 - $74,999
- ☐ over $75,000

5. What are the ages of the children living in your house?
- ☐ 0 - 14
- ☐ 15+

6. Marital Status
- ☐ Single
- ☐ Married
- ☐ Divorced
- ☐ Widowed

7. How did you find out about the book?
(please choose one)
- ☐ Recommendation
- ☐ Store Display
- ☐ Online
- ☐ Catalog/Mailing
- ☐ Interview/Review

8. Where do you usually buy books?
(please choose one)
- ☐ Bookstore
- ☐ Online
- ☐ Book Club/Mail Order
- ☐ Price Club (Sam's Club, Costco's, etc.)
- ☐ Retail Store (Target, Wal-Mart, etc.)

9. What subject do you enjoy reading about the most?
(please choose one)
- ☐ Parenting/Family
- ☐ Relationships
- ☐ Recovery/Addictions
- ☐ Health/Nutrition
- ☐ Christianity
- ☐ Spirituality/Inspiration
- ☐ Business Self-help
- ☐ Women's Issues
- ☐ Sports

10. What attracts you most to a book?
(please choose one)
- ☐ Title
- ☐ Cover Design
- ☐ Author
- ☐ Content

TAPE IN MIDDLE; DO NOT STAPLE

BUSINESS REPLY MAIL

FIRST-CLASS MAIL PERMIT NO 45 DEERFIELD BEACH, FL

POSTAGE WILL BE PAID BY ADDRESSEE

Health Communications, Inc.
3201 SW 15th Street
Deerfield Beach FL 33442-9875

FOLD HERE

Comments

7

Show Me the Money

What Does Money Mean to You?

Most people spend so much of their lives worrying about money: the management, earning and lack of money. Others claim to have no interest in money whatsoever, but this is often because they think it's so much hassle that they can't be bothered to master it, and so they ignore their finances as much as possible while still keeping body and soul together.

Do you disdain dealing with money? Are you to money what Marilyn Monroe was to digging trenches? Marilyn would have claimed no interest at all in trenches, because it wasn't her thing; but with money, it's everyone's thing—we all need money to survive.

And of course, we're not about digging trenches; we're about building skyrockets.

We all need money to survive.

How worried are you about money right now?

a) Completely not bothered.

b) Somewhat concerned.

c) Stressed out.

d) So freaked that you want to go sell this book to get some cash.

Money worries take numerous forms and can include not having enough change for the bus; having to make this month's payment on the villa in the Swiss Alps; business expenses exceeding income; inadequate pension funding; not enough for basics or small luxuries; inflation; too little to cover times of illness or unemployment; not enough to feed, clothe and educate the kids; never earning enough to lead the lifestyle to which you aspire—in fact, money seems to impact on most areas of our lives.

So what exactly is this "money" that has the vast majority of the world's population in such a tizzy?

Money is a token of the exchange of energy. You provide a product or service and are given money to the supposed or agreed value of that service. The token can then be exchanged for other services or products of the same value. In the past people used to barter, which could be a fairly complicated business as you often had to find someone who had exactly the chicken, bucket, hoe, donkey and pigskin of wine that you wanted to swap for your plowing oxen. So it's obvious that money is a wonderfully practical invention.

Do you feel that you are in control of this exchange of energy?

There are those of you who are always wishing that more money would come your way in the form of a lottery win, business break, insurance claim, inheritance and so on, while at the same time believing you are not deserving of extreme wealth, that it will never be a part of your life, that you are destined to struggle along to your deathbed unless there is some magical intervention from outside.

Newsflash: riches are your birthright! The transformation starts here.

Riches are your birthright.

What Is Money?

There are so many clichés attached to money which people subconsciously incorporate into their belief systems and then act on the basis of those beliefs. (For example, if you start to believe that money doesn't grow on trees, you might become overly cautious to the point of paralysis.) Some of those clichés are:

"Money makes the world go around."
"Money is the root of all evil."
"Money can't buy you love."
"A dollar saved is a dollar earned."
"The rich get richer, and the poor get poorer."
"Money doesn't grow on trees."

Think for a moment, what other clichés occur to you?

In fact, money is whatever you believe it is. If you believe that it's an empowering force for good, then it is. If you believe that it's a crippling pain in the neck, then it is just that for you.

Money is whatever you believe it is.

TASK

Let's explore what you believe to be true about money.

Think back to when you were growing up. What was the attitude toward money of those around you?

Write down memories of receiving, giving, earning, losing and pilfering money:

_____

_____

_____

_____

_____

What did you specifically hear regarding money from those around you as you grew up? Some suggestions:

"Money is a necessary evil."

"There's never enough money."

"My money is as good as anyone else's."

"Don't waste money."

"The rich take care of the poor."

"The poor make money for the rich."

"The more you earn the more the tax man gets."

_____

_____

_____

_____

_____

What do you believe to be true about money now?

Circle all the following phrases that you believe to be true, even if they seem to contradict each other:

"Poverty is something to be ashamed of."

"Money should never be spoken of outside the family."

"Money should never be spoken of within the family."

"Robbing from the rich to give to the poor is harmless or noble."

"Money is made to go around."

"Look after the pennies, and the dollars will take care of themselves."

"The money will arrive somehow, from somewhere."

"The Lord will provide."

"The man is the breadwinner."

"Making money is child's play."

"Spending money is child's play."

"Wealthy people are deceitful, obsessive or lucky."

"Poor people are lazy or never got a good start in life."

"Poverty is freedom."

"Poverty is a ball and chain."

"Wealth is freedom."

"Wealth is a ball and chain."

"I will always be in debt."

"I'm not good with budgets."

"Money kills relationships."

"I will never make enough money to be comfortable."

"I will be a millionaire one day."

"I am a great saver."

"I couldn't save a penny in my current circumstances."

Other beliefs:

_____

_____

_____

_____

_____

_____

ⓦ ⓦ ⓦ ⓦ ⓦ

Limiting
beliefs about
money lead
to limiting
amounts of
money.

ⓦ ⓦ ⓦ ⓦ ⓦ

Limiting beliefs about money lead to limiting amounts of money. If you believe you can't possibly save money, then you won't. Take someone with the same amount of income and expenses as you, and if that person has a belief that they CAN save money, they will find a way—even though you thought it couldn't be done. (See "Fantasize Your Future," chapter two.)

ⓐ ⓐ

You and Your Money

How could a lack of money be affecting your life right now? Is there someone you love who you are unable to help or visit because of a cash-flow problem? Are Christmas and birthdays a bit of a strain? Are you still driving that old beater or taking public transportation out of necessity? Are you stuck in the house most evenings? Are your children doing without? Do you have to buy cheap, generic, processed foods? Is your house in need of expensive TLC? Do you have to work exorbitant hours just to keep things steady?

TASK ௯

Write down exactly the ways in which your life is curtailed by not having ample money at your disposal:

_____

_____

_____

_____

_____

_____

_____

_____

How could your life be transformed by money?

~ You could provide for those you love and be able to donate significantly to your favorite charities.

~ You could plan your life according to your wishes rather than having it dictated by your needs.

~ If you suddenly needed medical attention, you could immediately and easily pay for the very best care.

~ You could take vacations to any part of the world.

~ You could live in your dream home and drive your dream car.

~ You could decide to work only the hours you wanted to.

௯ ௯

TASK ๑

Write in detail how your life would look if you had all the money you could ever need. Imagine the ultimate, the very extreme:

_____

_____

_____

๑ ๑ ๑ ๑ ๑ ๑
Rags to riches is a fairy tale that comes true for people around the world every day.
๑ ๑ ๑ ๑ ๑ ๑

Many people who now live this ultimate lifestyle started out with just as much as you, and sometimes with even less. Rags to riches is a fairy tale that comes true for people around the world every day.

Now decide what better beliefs will lead to your life of plenty. Suggestions:

~ I deserve massive amounts of money to fulfill all my dreams.

~ Whatever the circumstances, I can make money quickly, honestly and without breaking my back.

~ There is more than enough money in the world for everyone.

~ I will still be loved when I have money, but not because of the money.

~ I can save easily and effortlessly.

~ I appreciate all the luxuries money affords me.

~ Money is mine to keep and enjoy.

~ I create abundance wherever I go.

~ I enjoy sharing my wealth with others.

~ I love money.

The love of money is a contentious issue. We're not talking about focusing on money to the exclusion of all else, or being obsessive, addictive, mean or exploitative as a result of your relationship with money. We're talking about being passionate about the fantastic things that money can do for you and the great fun you can have creating a steady flow of wealth into your life. Loving money can mean being comfortable that money is working for you to the benefit of all those you come in contact with.

TASK

Write a list of your preferred beliefs in regard to money (if you resolve to stick with the old beliefs, realize that little or no positive change is likely to come about in your financial life as a result).

_____

_____

_____

_____

_____

_____

_____

_____

Take Action

Now that you have these new beliefs, it's time to take ACTION, to put your better beliefs to work. Use this chapter, in conjunction with the goal-fixing chapter three, to set specific financial goals based on what's discussed on the following pages.

For centuries people from Ireland thought of themselves as an impoverished nation. This "poverty mentality" was transformed with the economic boom of recent years, but with gloomy predictions for the Irish and global economies, people are in danger of reverting to old patterns of thinking negatively and defensively about money.

Booms are built largely on confidence. Confidence leads to individuals taking massive action on money-making ideas, which in turn leads to massive results. So it's important to stay strong and stick by your empowering beliefs. Even in down-turning economies there are plenty of people making big profits and earning large salaries. Make sure you're in the right mindset to be one of these.

Stay strong and stick by your empowering beliefs.

The opposite of confidence is fear. Fear is a big factor for many people when it comes to money. Fear of the bills and statements arriving at the doormat, fear of meeting the bank manager, fear of not being able to pay for your round in the pub, fear of making a mistake in your accounting, fear that you have overextended your resources, fear of falling further and further into debt.

For some, this fear is more of a constant, mild anxiety than an out-and-out terror, but even this anxiety is an unnecessary infringement on your life.

Most fears stem from a lack of knowledge, information, understanding or a definite plan. Many people have no idea what their weekly, monthly and annual income and expenses are. Many have no idea how much money they owe or how much of their mortgage has been repaid.

TASK

It's time to take a good look at your money and remember that the best way out is always through. In order to make money you have to focus on it.

Take out all your pay stubs, balance sheets, loan agreements, IOUs and any other receipts or bits of financial information you might have. Using these, piece together a picture of what money comes into your life, what money goes out, and what you owe and are owed.

Write out how much you earn every month and how much you spend for essentials such as rent, food and utilities, and for luxuries such as entertainment. At the very least the money coming in should exceed the money going out. With an annual expense such as a vacation, divide the figure by twelve to discover how much this vacation costs you per month. If you buy a newspaper six days a week, multiply the cost by

In order to make money you have to focus on it.

twenty-four to discover the monthly cost. Do not leave anything out no matter how trifling it may seem. One pack of popcorn per week adds up to fifty dollars over a year, and one cinema ticket per month adds up to over a hundred dollars a year.

Only when you have written out all the money in and out, and all the money owing and owed, can you set up a viable plan of action for earning, saving, repaying and spending.

EXAMPLE

Aidan, a client who initially came to us for coaching about relationships and health, did this exercise and was shocked to discover that he was fifteen thousand dollars in debt, twice what he thought he owed. He had two maxed-out credit cards, owed small sums to his parents and a friend, and had a car loan from the bank. As a result of this discovery, he decided to make drastic changes in his expenditures and find ways to make more money. The impetus for these changes came directly as a result of being faced with the facts. After the initial stomach lurch, he put in place a plan of action and immediately felt in control of the situation.

So it's clear that not only businesses have to look at balance sheets and work out how much money they'll need to take in. You should think of yourself as a minicorporation so you don't live your life blind to the financial road ahead.

෧ ෧

Money Crisis

If you are in money crisis right now, you might want to consider the following steps:

1. Talk to your bank manager and other available institutions about the best ways to proceed.

2. Debt consolidation, as strongly advocated on TV commercials and the Internet, is not usually a good idea, as it prolongs the repayment, resulting in a large increase in the interest you pay. If you have a five-year car loan and you consolidate it with a fifteen-year mortgage, you are now paying your car off over fifteen years, which is an expensive thing to do. It might seem like a stress-free way to control your debt, but it's a short-term fix to a long-term problem. Work out a way to pay off your debts in a shorter amount of time instead. Being debt free is the first step to financial freedom.

   ❀ ❀ ❀ ❀ ❀

   Being debt free is the first step to financial freedom.

   ❀ ❀ ❀ ❀ ❀

3. If your finances are simply a bit messy, concentrate on putting some money aside as savings and getting completely debt free. Most important is paying off the high-interest credit card bills. Keep only one credit card for emergencies, the lowest-interest-rate card available, and if you do have to use it in an emergency, pay off the bill even before it arrives on your doorstep. Cut up all old credit cards. Becoming debt free may not be possible

immediately, but there are often ways to speed up the repayment process or pay off loans with higher interest rates more quickly.

If your finances are in great shape, congratulations! Its time to get yourself to a place where you never have to work another day in your life unless you choose to, while still affording all the dream luxuries available in the world. Everyone can get to this place eventually, regardless of their starting points, and you lucky people have a head start.

Earning Money

If you have discerned from this exercise that you need to make more money, you must realize that it's not necessarily about getting a raise or working harder, it's about getting smarter about your attitude toward earning, keeping and creating money.

If you have a basic salary, ensure that you are receiving what you feel you are worth according to the market. Refer to "Amazing Careers and How to Get There," chapter five, for more information on this subject.

If you are in business, ask yourself if you are milking your business to the maximum or merely taking home the obvious cream?

EXAMPLE

Someone who runs a small gift shop could make money by:

~ Selling the gifts from the shop in the traditional way.

~ Selling the gifts on the Internet.

~ Charging people for advertising on the gift-shop Web site.

~ Taking a percentage of the profit of the products people sell when the customer has gone to their website via the gift-shop website.

~ Renting the unused storage space out back to an amateur dramatics society for rehearsals or scenery and costume storage.

~ Renting space in the front of the gift shop to an ice-cream vendor during the summer months.

~ Lending inventory out to film companies and photographers for a per-item fee.

If you do not own a business, it's far more difficult to make extra income in this way. So it's worth thinking about what type of business you might like to set up, even on a part-time basis.

Keeping Money

It's easier to *keep* a dollar than it is to *earn* a dollar. When you earn money you must pay taxes on it, so for every dollar you keep, you have to earn roughly a dollar and a half. Set up a savings system right now, putting a minimum of ten percent of all the money you receive into a savings account. This account is sacred and must not be dipped into except for purposes of investment. You'll find you won't miss it from your spending budget.

It's easier to keep a dollar than it is to earn a dollar.

Also set aside enough money so that if you were to fall ill or have to leave work for whatever reason, all your expenses will be covered for a minimum of two months. This rainy day money should always sit in a secure bank, credit union or brokerage account where you have instant access to it.

If you are self-employed or run a business, it is imperative that you have a professionally set up accounting system and that you keep your business and personal accounts separate. However, don't just blindly trust the advice of accountants and business managers. It's important to educate yourself as to the financial dealings in your business.

So what do you do with your personal savings once you have them?

Savings Accounts

Leaving your money in the bank, even in a very high-yield, long-term savings account (i.e., where you can't take your money out for five years, and in that time it gives you 4.5 percent interest or more) will rarely mean that your money even keeps up with inflation. Savings accounts are a place to put your money for a short amount of time before you move it to a place where it can start to make money for you.

Stocks, Bonds and Real Estate

The best returns on investments since World War II have been stocks, bonds and real estate. These are such huge subjects that it's well worth your time and money to buy recommended books on the subjects and attend seminars. Here are some we highly recommend:

Rich Dad Poor Dad, by Robert Kiyosaki and
   Sharon Lechter, Warner Business Books, 2000.
Multiple Streams of Income, by Robert G. Allen,
   John Wiley & Sons, 2004.
Getting Started in Trading, by Sunny J. Harris,
   John Wiley & Sons, 2000.

However, we must stress that you should not trade directly on the stock exchange until you are thoroughly versed in what you are doing and have been trading a paper portfolio for a few months, which means trading as if you were buying shares while not actually doing so.

Many people have lost large amounts of money buying telecom stocks, for instance. Many of these investors trusted in the IPO price, and trusted that the price would continue to rise. If they had done a little more research, they might have discovered that telecom IPOs have a habit of rising steeply at first and then falling, and they might have decided that the stock was overpriced in the first place. Good investors will do their own research and not risk all their savings in a single investment.

We do not recommend that you rush off and give your savings to a broker to invest for you. Many brokers charge big commissions, and despite the fact that it is their job to be so, many are not skilled at investing in the stock market.

Investment Clubs

Thousands of people get good experience in investing through joining an investment club. Check out the Internet, and do some research as to what clubs might suit you. We strongly recommend that you educate yourself on every aspect of investing, and then start to invest in a smart way that works best for you.

Mentoring

It is an excellent idea to find yourself a mentor or guide in this instance. If you can talk at length with someone who has been successful in buying and selling stocks, bonds and real estate, he or she will be a mine of information as to whether the market is good to get into right now, what the pitfalls might be and so on.

With investing, as with career choices, it's vital to find your passion. Some people love buying and selling property, others love buying bonds or shares, others love buying collectables such as antiques, while the braver among us love nothing better than trading options.

How are *you* going to make *your* money?

With investing, as with career choices, it's vital to find your passion.

Spending

In order to have something to invest, you need to watch your spending habits.

TASK 🌀🌀🌀🌀🌀🌀🌀🌀🌀🌀🌀🌀🌀🌀🌀🌀🌀🌀🌀🌀🌀🌀🌀🌀🌀

Write down everything you've bought recently that wasn't a necessity:

_____

_____

_____

_____

_____

How important were these items to you at the time of purchase? Why did you buy them? How important have they been to you since the purchase? What emotional needs have they been serving since the start?

"Retail therapy" is a popular and catchy term used to describe a behavior that can be considered a valuable way of nurturing yourself and feeling good (mend your broken heart with a Fendi, darling). There are many ways in which you can nurture yourself and feel better, but buying things you don't need or can't afford is not a savvy approach. "Retail therapy" can be reckless and bankrupting, and although it might give a short-term high or feeling of relief, before long the old, underlying problem reemerges. For some, shopping becomes a serious addiction and has been the cause of marital break-ups, foreclosures on homes and suicide.

Various sums of money disappear regularly from our lives without us even noticing.

🌀🌀🌀🌀🌀🌀🌀🌀🌀🌀🌀🌀🌀🌀🌀🌀🌀🌀🌀🌀🌀🌀🌀🌀🌀

TASK ᕙᕙᕙᕙᕙᕙᕙᕙᕙᕙᕙᕙᕙᕙᕙᕙᕙᕙᕙᕙ

As you answer these questions, work out roughly the number of minutes, hours or days it would take you to earn the sum of money in question.

- ~ How many times do you take a chance on being ticketed by parking illegally?
- ~ How many times do you make peak-time cell phone calls instead of using a landline at night?
- ~ How often do you pay for classes and not show up or pay for magazines and never read them?
- ~ How much food do you throw out every week because you haven't properly planned your purchases?
- ~ What other ways do you fritter money away cent by cent?

ᕙᕙᕙᕙᕙᕙᕙᕙᕙᕙᕙᕙᕙᕙᕙᕙᕙᕙᕙᕙᕙᕙ

Save Money Right Now

TASK ᕙᕙᕙᕙᕙᕙᕙᕙᕙᕙᕙᕙᕙᕙᕙᕙᕙᕙᕙᕙ

Here are some improvements you can make right now to save money:

- ~ Get hooked up to the Internet to stay in touch, rather than spending hours on the phone talking long-distance to friends and relatives.

- Buy plane tickets and seasonal items as far as possible in advance.
- Write out a feasible expense budget for necessities and luxuries, and stick to it.
- Make a commitment to learn more about your money and how it can be put to work making more money for you.
- Have a meeting with the whole family and decide to be diligent about not wasting electricity, completely filling the dishwasher, turning off lights and so on.
- Comparison shop. Two minutes on the phone can save you anything from a few cents to hundreds of dollars.
- Ask for discounts on big-ticket items with private dealers. Usually you will receive one just for asking. Paying full price for a freezer, sofa or car is crazy. Simply ask, "What discount can I get on that?"
- Add as many more instant money savers as you can think of here:

- _____
  _____
- _____
  _____
- _____
  _____
- _____
  _____

Money, says the proverb, makes money.
When you have got a little, it is often easy to get more.

—CHARLES DICKENS

Surplus wealth is a sacred truth which
its possessor is bound to administer in his lifetime
for the good of the community.

—ANDREW CARNEGIE

If money is your hope for independence
you will never have it. The only real security that
a man will have in this world is a reserve of
knowledge, experience and ability.

—HENRY FORD

I think it is a man's duty to make all the
money he can, to keep all that he can,
and give away all that he can.

—JOHN D. ROCKEFELLER SR.

But remember the Lord your God, for it is he
who gives you the ability to produce wealth.

—DEUTERONOMY 8:18

A banker is a fellow who lends you his umbrella
when the sun is shining and wants it back
the minute it starts to rain.

—MARK TWAIN

There are people who have money
and people who are rich.

—GEOFFREY CHAUCER

I conceive that the great part of
the miseries of mankind are brought upon
them by false estimates they have
of the value of things.

—BENJAMIN FRANKLIN

If you want to feel rich, just count all of the
things you have that money can't buy.

—ANONYMOUS

Money is like manure.
You have to spread it around or it smells.

—J. PAUL GETTY

Beware of little expenses.
A small leak will sink a great ship.

—BENJAMIN FRANKLIN

Of all the icy blasts that blow on love,
a request for money is the most chilling
and havoc wreaking.

—GUSTAVE FLAUBERT

The two most beautiful words in the English
language are: "Check Enclosed."

—DOROTHY PARKER

Ordinary riches can be stolen;
real riches cannot. In your soul are infinitely
precious things that cannot be
taken from you.

—OSCAR WILDE

Prosperity is a great teacher;
adversity a greater.

—WILLIAM HAZLITT

That some should be rich shows that
others may become rich, and hence is just
encouragement to industry
and enterprise.

—ABRAHAM LINCOLN

8

Fantastic Relationships

The Need to Relate

Unless you live inside a hole in an abandoned cave in the middle of a wilderness with wild man-eating beasts roaming the perimeters, then you'll have relationships with people. Even then, the IRS would probably find you for a chat!

You might be the type of person who gets along with everyone, but even those who are satisfied with how they relate to others can benefit from looking at their good relationships and creating new ties. Or perhaps you think you're just not a "people person." The fact of the matter is that people need people, so it's best to tap into your god-given ability to relate effectively. The first step to ensuring that you enjoy the best in your relationships is to look at how you act, and interact, with regard to others.

151

We relate to people in many different ways—as colleagues, parents, siblings, lovers, children, acquaintances, customers, passers-by, friends. In fact, most people could find a different term to describe their connection to each person they know.

Relationships are an unparalleled opportunity for loving, laughing and learning. And yet many people in the world make themselves frustrated and miserable by wanting those around them to act in a certain way, by setting rules and one-sided expectations on relationships:

> "If my mother could be more interested in my life, then I'd be much happier."
> "If only the anchor man or woman would smile every now and then, my morning would get off to a brighter start."
> "If my coworkers weren't so grumpy all the time, I'd be a more positive person."
> "If the other drivers stopped hogging the fast lane at thirty miles an hour, my drive home would be far more relaxing."
> "If my husband really listened to me, then I'd feel more cherished and understood and wouldn't eat so many chocolate cookies."
> "If my children cleaned their rooms, I'd be in a better mood."
> "If my boss would stop piling on the work, I wouldn't get so stressed."

You can't control the people you're in relationships

with; you can only control who you are and what you bring to that relationship.

Taking Responsibility

Rather than waiting for someone to act according to your rules and expectations, it's vital to take responsibility for what you do and what you don't do, what you say and what you don't say. Decide that you're going to feel cherished, even if your husband isn't listening as attentively as you might wish for. Trust that other people are also doing the best they know how, and giving as much as they can, based on what they are going through. That's a pretty unpopular concept as people these days usually want to ensure that they're getting as much as they're giving. It's important to remember that other people have the right to do things as they see fit, even if this doesn't exactly mesh with your view of the relationship. If you feel that someone in the relationship needs changing, you could be right—that person is you. If you do get others to change to make you happy, it's highly probable that you'll soon notice something else you want to change about them, and loving relationships can turn into improvement battlefields. Change starts and continues with you.

Other people have the right to do things as they see fit.

Two main factors affect all your relationships:

1. YOUR ACTIONS—You can take responsibility to communicate what you want.
2. YOUR BELIEFS—Although you can't control what you get from the relationship, you can control the way to react to, or think about, the relationship.

Change starts and continues with you.

1. Your Actions

Let's look first at your communication skills. There are always several ways of saying the same thing, and we want you to choose the most effective. Broadly speaking, you can communicate:

a) badly: "You never the wash the car." (This might be read as a criticism rather than a request.)
b) sloppily: "The car is really dirty." (This might seem to be a hint but could be taken as a soft criticism or an observation.)
c) effectively: "Would you wash the car, please?" (Most likely to be taken as a request. But if repeated without change, could become a nag.)

Obviously the most effective way to get the car washed is to ask politely and pay attention to the response.

The Power of Words

People often don't realize the negative and positive power their words can have on people. We say things in order to get some response (a kind word, an action, a certain emotional reaction from the listener, an understanding, a listening ear, clarity of purpose and so on), and we want the best possible outcome from what we say. This means choosing carefully the best words and not just hoping that, "Ah, sure they'll know what I mean."

What would you understand by the question, "What are you doing tonight?"

~ That you're being asked out on a date?
~ That someone wants you out of the house?
~ That someone wants some quality time with you?

There are loads of interpretations to this one phrase. What ways could the following phrases be taken?
"What do you mean by that?"
"No, it's fine. Don't worry about it."
"Whatever."

It's clear how easy it is for people to misunderstand each other, especially if sarcasm is employed liberally. As a great communicator, it's imperative that what you communicate reaches the other person as intact as it was when it left your brain, not as a different idea or intention. If you give out roses, you want them to arrive as roses and not as nettles. You must be alert to the effect your words are having. Even as English speakers, even as members of the same family, we do not all speak the same language.

You must be alert to the effect your words are having.

Tone

The *tone* we adopt to communicate words is just as important as the words themselves, if not more so. You can use a harsh, soft, gentle, seductive, sympathetic, coarse, tense, demanding or chirpy tone.

TASK 🌀 🌀 🌀 🌀 🌀 🌀 🌀 🌀 🌀 🌀 🌀 🌀 🌀 🌀 🌀 🌀 🌀 🌀 🌀

Try this. Say the sentence, "Would you wash the car, please?" using all of the tones just listed, and hear the difference that is communicated with each tone choice. (Please do it! Sitting there nodding your head won't really get you to understand this. Play along; it's fun!)

What have you learned from this exercise?

Now ask yourself this: What are the *three* dominant tones in your life? Are they whiny, melodious, grating, bombastic, wary, mellow . . . ?

Now that you have identified your *dominant* tones, how do you think you can change your tonality in a way that improves your communication? What would be easier for others to listen to? If you make it easy for people to listen to you, you have a far better chance of achieving your communication aim.

It's also worth paying attention to the *speed, volume* and *emphasis* of your speech.

🌀 🌀

Breathing and Control

You'll find that your *breathing* has a huge effect on all these aspects of your communication mastery. Shallow breaths leave room for very little control. Breathe deeply (from your diaphragm), and notice how much easier it is to get your point across.

Communicator Tricks

Other great communicator tricks that work well:

- ~ Count to *five* before jumping in with an opinion. This way you won't stomp all over the other person's view.
- ~ Don't hold back either. Always ensure that you say something you want to say rather than holding back through fear or laziness.
- ~ If you're not exactly sure what someone means, ask for clarity rather than assuming the worst.
- ~ Lower your eyebrows before you start to speak. This relaxes your facial muscles, leading to better voice control.
- ~ Really listen to the other person, rather than focusing on the next thing you're going to say.
- ~ Pay attention to your posture and gestures. Body language is the greatest communicator of all, so make sure your body isn't contradicting what's coming out of your mouth. If you're saying, "I love you," but your arms and legs are crossed defensively and your body is turned away from the other person, the words won't have quite the same effect.

2. Your Beliefs

What you believe to be true about the relationship is the second important factor.

Here are some typical beliefs people might have about their relationships:

"He'll probably leave me one day; they usually do."

"We're soul mates."

"The children are my world."

"My mother always preferred my sister. I was always the odd child."

"My boss couldn't run the place without me."

Although you may be able to rationalize your belief in any of the above, realize that your generalization about a relationship isn't necessarily the absolute truth. Maybe your mother didn't prefer your sister and thought of you as an adventurous, creative child, rather than an odd one. Wanting more of your mother's attention over the years, you may have built up a belief about the relationship that served your fear of not getting the same amount of love. Does this belief help you? If not, let it go, and get a new, better belief.

EXAMPLES

OLD BELIEF—"My family is holding me back; they always want me to do things for them."

BETTER BELIEF—"My family trusts and appreciates me and supports anything I want to do in my life."

OLD BELIEF —"People are out to cheat you at every turn."

BETTER BELIEF—"People are honest despite one or two bad apples."

TASK ⊚

Check out all your beliefs and see whether they are in any way restricting you from enjoying your relationships. On one page write down (in blue or black ink) three or more restricting beliefs with regard to:

1) family
2) friends
3) work colleagues
4) people in general

On the next page write down (in red, green or purple ink) your corresponding preferred beliefs.

Once that's done, take the restricting beliefs page and rip it up into the tiniest pieces, making snowflake confetti of it. Go out to the yard, beach or park, and scatter it.

Then put on your favorite uplifting piece of music, and read aloud from your new empowering belief page. Let yourself go; dance around freely; be natural and passionate as you embrace your triumph over the negative in your relationships. While you're still in that "great state," find someone who's on your list and be with them in that new way. Don't get disheartened if you fall into the same old patterns and habits. Cut yourself some slack, and just keep focusing on the new way, the things you want to believe.

If you think it could help you, show the people concerned what you've written, without expectation. When

⊚ ⊚ ⊚ ⊚ ⊚

Embrace your triumph over the negative.

⊚ ⊚ ⊚ ⊚ ⊚

you make a statement, you are putting yourself in a position where it's more difficult not to follow through.

❀ ❀

Statement of Intent

It's invaluable to know what you expect, and what is expected of you, in a relationship. People don't usually think in terms of having relationship goals, unless it's a goal like "get married," "stop arguing," or "live nearer to each other."

When you define the ways in which you would like the relationship to get better, you're more likely to be successful than if you merely have a fuzzy notion of what "a better relationship" might be like. Most companies now have mission statements that ensure everyone is journeying using the same map. One form of mission statement in terms of personal relationships is the marriage vow.

There are monumental advantages to creating a statement of intent for each of your relationships. It focuses you on how you would ideally like to be in the relationship: your needs, wants, hopes and dreams, what you have to give. It brings you back to the important basics, gives a framework in which the relationship can mature and grow, demonstrates commitment, and defines roles and responsibilities.

Ideally, two people should write their statements together, but even writing them alone is of huge advantage to you both.

A Husband's Statement for His Relationship with His Wife

~ I will frequently ask my wife how I can best show her that I love and support her.

~ I will treat her like the goddess she is.

~ I will take time to listen and understand her sexual needs.

~ I will acknowledge, and act upon, the fact that sex is not only about *my* love, lust or gratification, but just as important, it is about my *wife's* love, lust and gratification.

~ When she is repeating a request, I will understand this means there is a need of hers that I am not yet fulfilling, rather than dismissing it as nagging.

~ I will take time for myself every weekend to work out and spend time with friends, without feeling guilty for leaving her at home.

~ I will communicate my ambitions to her so she remains part of my life-dream.

~ I will do my utmost to take care of all her needs, even when I don't understand them.

~ I will tell her in as many ways as I can, as often as I can, how grateful I am to have her in my life.

~ I will ensure that I know her sexual fantasies and will surprise her appropriately.

~ I will maintain a good emotional state even if she is in a bad mood.

~ I will listen to what she is saying and contribute
to the conversation in order to keep the communication channels open.

~ I will equally share in the household tasks rather
than just helping out.

~ When we are in public, I will make sure everyone knows that she is the most special woman
in the room.

~ I will seek her out when I get home from work,
give her a genuine loving hug and plan some
time for later that evening when we can discuss
our days.

~ I will let her know in what I say and do that we
are both in this together forever.

(The above statement could equally be written by a
wife for her husband.)

A Daughter's Statement for Her Relationship with Her Mother

~ I will take time to understand what my mother
is feeling and thinking, rather than assuming I
know it all.

~ When she compliments, praises and supports
me, I will accept this gratefully.

~ I will ask myself what I can do for her rather
than always looking for comfort and understanding from her.

~ I will ask her more about her life and
experiences.

~ I will listen to her advice even if I choose not to act upon it.

~ I will respect her always, never belittling or talking down to her.

~ I will hug her regularly.

~ I will not wreck my head trying too hard to make things perfect between us.

~ I will realize there is no need to tell her all my plans and dreams or to get her approval for my life.

~ I will stop relating every tiny supposed disaster and difficulty back to her.

~ I will remind myself that she needs as much attention as I do.

~ I will not crumble when I feel she has criticized me.

~ I will act according to my current age and experience rather than reverting to childhood behaviors.

~ I will make sure she is always a part of my life while not being my whole life.

A Son's Statement for His Relationship with His Father

~ I will be curious about his life as a little boy and young man.

~ I will listen without judgement.

~ I will always respect him.

~ I will invite him out socially to be with my friends.

~ I will ask him what he would like me to do for him.

~ I will surprise him in positive, unique ways.

~ I will exercise more tolerance, knowing that one day I may be a father (if not already).

~ I will remember that his years carry much wisdom, and I will endeavor to learn as much as I can from him.

~ I will ask him for a list of his most-used quotes.

~ I will write a journal of his life.

Your statements are covenants to be cherished and acted upon. From time to time, review your statements of intent in order to remind yourself about what you want in the relationship and the ways it can be further improved.

Working Strategy

All relationships hit trouble patches.

All relationships hit trouble patches. Human beings are complex; they feel different things at different times, have different beliefs about the way things are or should be; they have different rules for the way the game should be played. Because there are no relationship referees on board every day, it's wise to set down some solutions to problems in advance.

Some relationship difficulties crop up frequently and can be quite easily resolved with a little forethought.

Rules and Guidelines

If someone is always hogging the TV remote control, why not have an agreed-upon strategy?

EXAMPLE

~ One person has jurisdiction over the TV on Monday, another on Tuesday, and so on.

~ Record one program if there is a clash.

~ Get the TV guide and have each person highlight what they want to watch so the viewing is more fairly distributed.

~ Agree that no one can switch channels if someone else is watching a show—no matter who is holding the remote.

It may sound obvious, but having a few guidelines and agreements in place prevents a lot of arguments. If you try to come up with solutions during the conflict, the atmosphere can be too heated and nonproductive.

Other household regulations can include filling the dishwasher in turns, each person folding their own laundry and placing dirty clothes in the laundry basket, and so on.

Relationships are about finding out what works for everyone involved and feeling good about it. This way people are responsible for their own actions and are accountable to those with whom they've agreed upon the rules. Sticking by the rules should be part of your statement of intent. This way nobody's boundaries are encroached.

Dealing with Arguments

Creating rules for how you're going to construct an argument is vital:

~ No one will storm out.

~ No one will raise his or her voice.

~ No one will bring past conflicts into the argument.

~ Problems will be resolved before bedtime.

~ Sentences will be started with "I feel," rather than the more accusatory "You did this," or "You always," or "You never . . ."

~ No swearing.

~ No one will bottle things up and build resentment.

~ Things will be said in a caring rather than sarcastic tone.

~ Each person will have a clear five minutes in which to speak without being interrupted.

Whatever works for you and your relationship. If things get too heated and one of you starts to sing, it can be a great way to change the focus from the negative back to an improved atmosphere. This does not demean the issue that you need resolved; it just puts it into a different perspective where it might be more easily dealt with. Nothing is ever fully resolved in tension and anxiety.

Nothing is ever fully resolved in tension and anxiety.

Bear the following in mind during times when good communication is essential:

~ Paraphrase back what you believe the other person is saying.

~ Face each other.

~ Be encouraging.

~ Don't blame or victimize.
~ Think of your words before you say them.
~ Be specific.
~ Be responsible.
~ Be assertive
~ Stick to the truth.
~ Stick to facts, and do not invent stories.
~ Lose the drama.

TASK

Brainstorm the following:

1. In the past, what solutions to disagreements have really worked for you?
2. What methods repeatedly don't work for you when you try to solve your relationship difficulties?
3. What have you never tried before, but have noticed has been successful for friends, colleagues or people on talk shows?
4. What can you decide on in advance that will resolve relationship problems more quickly and more to the satisfaction of everyone involved?
5. Do whatever you have to do to ensure that you adhere to the new methods of communication. For you, this might mean writing down the commitment (i.e., "I will count to ten and remind myself that I'm talking to a friend before I reply

to something I strongly disagree with"), or it might mean telling someone or even skywriting your resolve above the town. Congratulate yourself every time you communicate in your new, better way, and remember that it gets easier with repetition. Look forward to the improved relationships you will enjoy with everyone you come into contact with.

Substitution

Some people get so anxious around relationships that they inadvertently avoid connecting with people, shunning either distant or intimate relationships. They do this by focusing almost exclusively on hobbies, work, pets and household tasks—escaping contact with those around them. Sometimes the relationship substitution can be blatantly harmful, as people look for the solace, variety and connection that relationships usually provide through drink, drugs, unhealthy food, constant arguing or the sex industry.

Often the harm can be invisible, as the person indulging in this behavior can justify that they are doing the extra overtime, or whatever, for the benefit of their families anyway. However, ongoing disassociation from others is harmful, since human beings are not designed to be alone.

Ongoing disassociation from others is harmful.

We are all familiar with the old clichés of the man down at the pub, or up in the attic playing with his train set, while the woman sits downstairs reading a romance novel. Or someone mouthing, "I'm not in," when a friend phones and getting back to the TV. Or one worker hanging out in the storeroom rather than with coworkers.

It doesn't have to be an inanimate focus either; you can as easily avoid communicating with someone by spending time with another person as you can by spending time with the TV or train set. Mothers and fathers can fail to balance their attentions, giving an exorbitant amount of energy and time to the children while taking their partners for granted. People can also rely too heavily on the party atmosphere of a group rather than what they consider the drudgery of their home relationships. Women often get comfortable with women friends, where they gossip to keep the real world at bay.

Why do people pull back from other people? There are numerous reasons for doing this:

1. We feel we might be asked a particular question, or to perform a task or role, for which we aren't equipped.

2. We think the other person might influence us into having feelings that we aren't comfortable with at that time, such as feeling depressed, excited, bored, silly or impatient.

3. A belief that we are not good enough, which leads to feelings of inadequacy and stress around those we consider superior.

4. Inflated egos can lead us to think we'll be bored and have nothing to learn from others.

5. Believing we have nothing in common with people and being afraid that we just won't get along.

6. Believing that someone will hurt us.

7. Feeling resentful and simultaneously protecting ourselves and punishing the other person.

When people set up a consistent pattern of avoiding others, this is usually a sign of internal unrest. Another way of looking at this unrest is to understand that the feeling comes from fear. Although avoiding the situation brings temporary relief, the unrest or fear needs to be challenged radically so the relationship is not compromised permanently.

TASK

Really quickly and without thinking too hard, scribble down some answers to the following questions.

1. Who makes your heart sink when you know you have to meet with them?

_____

_____

2. Is there a social situation that you always try to avoid, such as family Christmas dinner, being stuck in an elevator with your boss or going out to dinner with your friends?

_____

_____

3. Who do you dissociate from; how and why?

_____

_____

ⓐ ⓐ

Boundaries

Although connecting to people is vitally important, it's also important to have your own space. If you allow people to constantly take your time, energy and attention without you deciding on your limits, you can end up becoming resentful and taking your necessary space in a destructive way. This can lead to you disassociating, as just discussed. Another way people deal unproductively with control over their boundaries is by starting to feel depressed, stressed, victimized, negative and overwhelmed.

Knowing your boundaries is about honoring yourself, about knowing when to bring certain people and situations closer, and about knowing when to pull away from them.

ⓐ ⓐ ⓐ ⓐ ⓐ ⓐ

Knowing your boundaries is about honoring yourself.

ⓐ ⓐ ⓐ ⓐ ⓐ ⓐ

TASK

Write out answers to the following questions so as to clarify your attitudes toward your boundaries.

1. What signs appear when you feel encroached upon? Do you:
   ~ Fold your arms?
   ~ Get a headache?
   ~ Look strained?
   ~ Zone out?
   ~ Bitch about the other person?
   ~ Make excuses and justifications?
   ~ Rush away?
   ~ Feel guilty?
   ~ Feel angry?
2. Would you hug someone you are meeting for the first time, or shake their hand? What about a family member?
3. Do you insist on quiet time after work to recoup your sense of self?
4. Would you discuss details of your life with the whole nation on a late-night talk show, with your friends, with your priest or with your partner?
5. Are you comfortable undressing in front of members of the same sex, or in front of your lover or spouse?
6. Will you let someone criticize you in public?
7. Do you know when you need a break from people?

8. How do you react when someone says or does something that disturbs or offends you? Do you:
   ~ Say nothing?
   ~ Make a huge fuss?
   ~ Tell everyone else?
   ~ Subtly get out of the situation?
   ~ Avoid that person or situation in the future?
   ~ Go with it and feel bad later?

⟋ ⟋

EXAMPLE

Jane was a young mother with time on her hands, money in her purse and a car—she was a party in search of a venue. She was a lovely woman but was driving her friend Susan to distraction, as she was always looking for her time and attention. Jane would phone Susan a few times a day and want to meet up, and if the answer was "no" she would often turn up anyway. Susan was a busy self-employed woman who felt that her time and space boundaries weren't being respected. She soon began to resent Jane and dread the daily phone calls. Rather than confronting the situation, Susan began to screen her calls and not answer the door when the bell rang. In the end she felt so uncomfortable that she initiated a huge fight about something else entirely in order to justify breaking off the friendship.

It would have been better had Susan acknowledged and respected her own boundaries from the start and let Jane know that she was uneasy with so much intense contact and that she needed specific space and time. Had she done so, there's a strong chance she would have been given what she needed and the friendship might still be intact today. If she had communicated to Jane that she would be far more comfortable speaking once a week and meeting up once every two weeks, there is every chance that Jane would have agreed. On the other hand, she might have continued to call incessantly, in which case Susan could have found a less volatile way to terminate the friendship.

Friendship does not have to be forever. If you've communicated what your boundaries are, and they still aren't being adhered to, it's worth radically distancing yourself rather than compromising yourself on an ongoing basis. People often think that formally ending a relationship is for love relationships only, but breaking up with poorly matched friends is sometimes the healthiest thing for both of you.

👁 👁 👁 👁 👁

Friendship does not have to be forever.

👁 👁 👁 👁 👁

EXAMPLE

Tim had just joined a new office and was happy when the guys invited him out for drinks after work. An hour or so into their night out, the conversation turned to women, and some of the men began to use really profane language when describing their wishful exploits with the fairer sex. Tim felt uneasy and offended by the language, but at first thought he'd just let it go, seeing as he was the new guy at the office. However, as they began to want to include him more in that part of the conversation, he spoke up. He smiled good-naturedly and said, "I'm really not into that kind of talk. You wouldn't even get that on *Jerry Springer*." His comment was challenged by one guy who said, "Come on, it's just a joke." To which Tim replied, "What are we, a group of kids?" Tim then went on to tell a story about a girl he'd recently met, in a way that was comfortable for him.

In the future they weren't so quick to speak in disrespectful or vulgar ways in front of him, and on the odd occasion when they did, Tim would take a break at the bar. By speaking up, Tim saved himself years of being part of conversations in which he wouldn't have been comfortable.

Insisting on the integrity of your boundaries is a habit you can either get into or out of. The more you preserve your boundaries, the stronger your integrity grows. It's all about doing what's right for you, about insisting that your own internal laws are respected without being overly dogmatic about it. These laws might change with time, but they should never be forced into change. Your boundaries are your human rights. That's why it's worth becoming acutely in tune with your comforts and discomforts around people.

It's all about doing what's right for you.

Don't ignore that feeling of discomfort; it's telling you something important. Also, don't make the mistake of focusing on how others are encroaching upon your personal space. Remember, it's entirely within your power to hold your space, your values and your comfort zone intact. People might inadvertently be making you feel uncomfortable, but it's your responsibility to communicate that. It's not their responsibility to guess at your boundaries. That's why it's important to get to know what your boundaries are rather than mixing them up with where other people expect your boundaries to be.

Love Relationships

There is an inordinate amount of hype and speculation around the whole issue of love. Magazines, radio and television shows are full of advice, dramatizations and gossip about him/her, him/him and her/her relationships. So as not to be swept away in the possible hysteria, it's important for you to realize that, although these relationships are more intense than nonsexual relationships, our same basic guidelines still apply.

Tips

Here are a few extra tips (should you need them) to catch you from tripping over at the first dating hurdles:

- ~ Don't immediately cast every person you meet in the role of possible "Dream Lover for Life."
- ~ Don't force other people to make decisions about you before they're ready.
- ~ Don't stay at home waiting for someone to show up. It's more than likely the pizza boy is not the one for you. So get out there to parties, clubs, friends' houses, and other social and sporting events.

~ Don't discuss your previous relationships with
   someone you've recently started going out with,
   especially if you're going to be negative.

~ Do respect that relationships have a natural
   rhythm that must fit in with the rhythms of the
   rest of your life. Taking things too quickly can
   interfere with this.

~ Do have fun rather than worrying whether a
   relationship is going to work out. It's not about
   getting to the finish line with someone, it's
   about having a great dance on the way.

~ Do break up with someone firmly but kindly
   when you realize that it's not working for you.
   It's also vital to let someone go graciously if they
   have taken the initiative to end the relationship.

~ Do trust your instincts over the advice of others,
   and always maintain your standards.

~ Do know in advance what type of person you
   want to be with so you don't end up
   compromising.

Connecting

TASK ⊘

Write the birthdays of all your close friends and
family. Beside each, write something you will do on
that day to make it special for them.

Suggestions:

~ Perhaps call them to tell a silly joke.
~ Secretly go to their house or place of work and wash their car.
~ Cook them a meal.
~ Find an item they've wanted for ages but have been having trouble locating, like a particular CD or a contact address for a long-lost friend.
~ Organize a surprise party.
~ Buy them something fun, like a minitrampoline or karaoke set.
~ Mend a rift in your relationship.
~ Have a request played for them on the radio.

Don't forget to include your own birthday—you're really special, too.

Name	Birthday	Special Action
_____	_____	_____
_____	_____	_____
_____	_____	_____
_____	_____	_____

Go through your phone book and call or drop a note to anyone you haven't spoken to in over three months. If you've decided it's best that you don't have that person in your life anymore, take them out of your book and place the contact information somewhere you can easily find it if you change your mind in the future.

Fun Time

As we grow older, we often start to restrict what we find fun. Sometimes it can become all about eating, drinking and watching TV shows.

Fun Task

As soon as possible, dedicate a whole day to having fun, using this list for ideas, as well as coming up with loads of your own. Pick *two* of these, and do them right now:

○ Go for a drive in a vintage car.
○ Make pancakes or chocolate Rice Krispies treats.
○ Blow bubbles.
○ Do a rain dance barefoot on the grass, even if it's already raining.
○ Hook up a swing.
○ Fish for minnows with jam jars.
○ Play a card game like solitaire—and cheat.
○ Splash in a puddle.

○ Wear two brightly colored odd socks.

○ Go outside and sing "Oh what a beautiful morning" in your best opera voice.

○ Spend the night in a teepee (with ten other people).

○ Drink your tea or coffee using an old china tea set.

○ Compose a jingle to promote yourself, and sing it in the shower or bath (or while you're doing your rain dance).

○ Write yourself a card about how great you are, then mail it to yourself.

○ Dance around the kitchen with a towel on your head to an old pop song.

○ Do a finger painting, and hang it on your wall.

○ Have Christmas in August.

○ Celebrate your birthday every six months (without the aging!).

○ Have your portrait done by a professional artist, caricaturist or photographer.

○ Join a donkey race.

○ Do a cartwheel, badly.

○ Find pictures in clouds and fires.

○ Go see a fortune teller, and tell them what's going to happen to you.

○ Make a dream list.

○ Have a theme coffee morning, where everyone has to be head-to-toe in red, or dress as each other, or as if shipwrecked on a desert island. Provide corresponding foods.

○ Make sculptures with your food at mealtimes. Devour them like the giant you are, letting all the guts and gore and tomato ketchup run down your face.

○ Make chicken noises.

○ Record yourself singing the current number-one song, and send it off to a major record company.

○ Call a shop to ask for information using a completely different accent.

○ Organize a three-legged race.

○ Go into a shop and try on an outfit that is completely different from your usual style—go ultra conservative or ultra wacky, and have fun with your reflection.

○ Play hangman, using only rude words.

9

Troubleshooting

Life Coaching Band-Aid Box

Damn, you've bought the book, you've read the book, and suddenly it's all going wrong!

In the event of crisis, here's your life-coaching Band-Aid box—to get you over those mountain-sized hiccups.

Procrastinating

Ever been a procrastinator? Do you find yourself putting things off?

EXAMPLE

If you are procrastinating about cleaning the basement, make the picture smaller! Initiate "the sloppy five minutes." Tell yourself you are going to tidy up the basement for five minutes and not going to do a particularly good job.

Worst possible scenario:

You shifted a few things around, and now you don't feel quite so guilty as you did five minutes ago.

Best possible scenario:

You shifted a few things, noticed how good it felt, got momentum going and blasted through the job.

We often procrastinate on something because the job seems too enormous, and we feel the need to do it perfectly. Stop being perfect; be fantastic and active instead. If something's worth doing, it's worth doing badly—you can make it better later.

Stop being perfect.

Always Making Excuses

Excuses can quickly become a bad habit and so much a part of our lives that we don't even notice them.

EXAMPLE

"I can't take on extra work because I am moving to a new house."

First, list the fears behind the excuses:

~ Fear of tiredness.
~ Fear of something being broken if you're not supervising.
~ Fear of failing on the work project.

Plan ahead to lessen these fears. To bust the fears:

~ Sleep well.
~ Wrap well.
~ Research well.

This excuse (I am moving to a new house) is a way of

legitimizing procrastinating about the action (taking on extra work). OK, so it's impossible—TRY IT ANYWAY!

Worst possible scenario:

You prove yourself right, and you reset the goal with a definite start time.

Best possible scenario:

You find that you can steal time, and you can get more done than you thought. Remember, if it has been done by anyone before, it can be done by you.

✪ ✪ ✪ ✪ ✪ ✪

If it has been done by anyone before, it can be done by you.

✪ ✪ ✪ ✪ ✪ ✪

EXAMPLE

"I can't be confident now, because I am too heavy."
List the fear behind the excuse:

~ People will notice me more if I act confident and might criticize my size.

This excuse (I am too heavy) is a way of legitimizing procrastinating about the action (being confident). OK, it's impossible—TRY IT ANYWAY!

Worst possible scenario:

You act confident for a period of time when you would otherwise have been nervous and unsure.

Best possible scenario:

You realize that you can be completely confident no matter how overweight you are, and you begin to get a greater kick out of life, possibly even leading to weight loss.

Overwhelm

When it all seems too much, too fast, too soon, "overwhelm" can make you feel stressed, exhausted and like throwing in the towel. Only there're too many towels, and none of them is the right size, and you don't have anywhere to throw them and. . . . Take time out. Go have a hot drink, talk to a majorly fun and easy-going person about anything except angst. Take yourself out on a date: go to the movies, walk on the beach, get a massage, do a favor for a friend. Notice that the sky is not falling in. Get everything back into perspective. It's only life after all, as the man said.

Take time out.

Taking time away from your thoughts is the key. Don't try to think of everything at once.

TASK

Get it all out of your head and onto paper. If you have it written down, you no longer have to carry it around in your head. Write down niggling problems, as well as what you want to achieve at work or around the house.

Ask yourself the following:

~ Have you been setting unrealistically high standards for yourself or others?

~ Have you been setting deadlines that are hard to meet?

~ Have you been failing to take adequate breaks?

Only go back to the tasks when you're back in a really good emotional state and armed with new strategies to make sure you don't get overwhelmed again.

Constant Self-Criticism

You may be unwittingly acting as your own worst critic. You know those little phrases that float around your head all day long? They have amazing power for good or bad.

Hearing voices is a pretty scary concept, and if the voices are telling you to kill the cat, you need to look beyond this book for help. On the other hand, they're probably telling you that you're useless; you can't do it; you're too old, too young, too fat, too skinny; you've made a fool of yourself; you'll never make it; this always happens to you; you're so stupid; everyone's talking about you; history is repeating itself; it's too good to be true; or _____

_____

(write your own favorite here).

These are the nasty, incessant little thoughts that sabotage your life. Why not turn them into voices that can greatly enhance your life instead?

First, notice what you're saying to yourself. Then change the tone you're saying it in. Try saying "I'm a worthless loser" in a really sexy voice and see how all the power is taken from the phrase.

Now change the statement to, "I'm fantastic. I'm really getting there," and try it in a Sean Connery or Marilyn Monroe voice. This will keep you aware of the fact that you're talking to yourself.

Sometimes, such as last thing at night or when you're supposed to be listening to someone else, you need to switch off the internal dialogue completely. You can't stop the thoughts, but you can be kind to them and watch them just drift by and move on. Don't ever fight with your thoughts; play with them, and watch them play. Become the peacemaker of your own head.

Become the peacemaker of your own head.

"There is nothing either good or bad but thinking makes it so." —William Shakespeare

Lack of Support

So you have all these great plans, and you're working excitedly toward them. But gradually you notice that others aren't as enthused as you are. Their eyes start to glaze over as they tap their fingers in Morse code for "Pulllease!" while you talk about your loft conversion. They say, "But most people lose money on the stock market" while you wax lyrical about investing. They tell you to pace yourself and not do so much, when all you want is to stay up half the night working on your pet project.

Why don't they understand? Don't they want you to succeed? They don't seem to care.

What you're really asking is: why can't they get into your mind and feel the way you do about your life?

Well they can't; it's impossible, unless you're the right type of alien from *Star Trek*, and it's not fair of you to expect this of them. Your task in this situation is to state clearly to the person precisely what you want from them. That's the only way of getting close to telepathy.

You might also want to consider that they are in fact supporting you, but just not showing it in a way you readily recognize. For some people, constructive criticism or silent appreciation is the highest form of being there for another. Communication is the key. Get specific.

Get specific.

EXAMPLES

Say:

"I want you to really listen to me when I tell you about my wishes and dreams, and I want you to verbally encourage me in these."

"I want you to take note of my small achievements, to communicate this to me and maybe to others also."

"I would feel more supported if you didn't criticize my plans or methods in that way. I love it when you tell me I've done something well."

"This project is more exciting to me when I feel you want to be involved."

It's important to be careful who you talk to. If you know you're going to get a negative response from a person, don't keep going back for more!

You have to become your own cheerleader. Once you are fully on your own side, it's time to find one other person who can get excited about your achievements in a way that you feel is supportive.

Accept that if you take people along your path, it's more likely to be by example. They'll sit in the new apartment, see you make money on your investments, and finally be really enthusiastic and ask you how you did it. The irony is that at this point you probably won't need their backing.

In order to get support, you've got to give some first. Do you get excited about what's going on in the lives of your family, friends and coworkers, or is your own life all-consuming to the detriment of anything else? Ask not what your thoughtless buddies can do for you, but what you can do for your thoughtless buddies.

Guilt

Guilt can close you down quicker than anything. Guilt is absolute hostility toward the self. Guilt feelings have many triggers: either something you have done or said, or something that has been done or said to you.

> Guilt is absolute hostility toward the self

Guilt triggers

1. If you're caught telling a lie, you feel awful that you're not being approved of and feel that you're a lesser person because you haven't lived up to your own values.

2. When you inadvertently hurt someone with

something you've said, your intention may not have been bad, but the result was painful.

3. If someone stands you up on a date, you can feel guilty, although the bad was done to you. You might feel that you're not good enough, or you were wrong to have expected anything in the first place, and you can use it as evidence to support the guilt you usually dredge up.

4. When you do something for yourself, you can often feel guilty that you haven't included others.

Ask yourself: would you be that harsh with a really good friend? Give yourself a break, and notice what you're learning. Guilt feelings are often proof of our feelings of inferiority. Why not deal with the insecurity rather than wallowing in the result?

Most guilt is something we have trained ourselves to feel, but it needn't exist if we don't let it.

Action

First take action.

1. OK, you've told a lie and done damage to yourself or others. Apologize and clean up your mess.

2. If you're suffering guilt even though your intention was good, realize that you can't be responsible for what goes on in other people's heads. To bring clarity to the situation you might want to explain your side without being defensive. This is life; there are constant misunderstandings. These can be sorted without emotional turmoil.

3. If you're feeling guilty for something someone else did, you're projecting your past guilt onto a present situation. Identify what that real guilt is about, and realize that you're experiencing emotional echoes. There is no point regurgitating guilt for the sake of it.

4. Think of yourself as a separate person outside yourself whose happiness and well-being is entirely your responsibility, and realize that everything you do for yourself ultimately does good for those around you.

Take stock

Ask yourself what you've learned from the situation. You might have learned that you have a particular fear which leads you to lie; you might have learned to be more sensitive to other people's feelings and your own; and finally you might have learned not to spend your hard-earned emotional dollars on a no-show or an also-ran!

Turn the bad feeling into a positive breakthrough in your own self-development. Thank yourself for the lesson, and move on.

If you see your guilt as a huge elephant, why not name the elephant, and put it somewhere safe, way in the back of your circus mind where it will be available if you really feel you need to visit it. Much better than carrying it around with you all the time. Best of all, don't keep elephants.

Can't Get Motivated

You *are* motivated. Even lying around the house takes motivation. When you slop around, you are motivated to feel good and avoid the stresses of life. So realize that whatever you are doing, you are already a motivated person. You just want to realign your motivation to more productive ends.

Remember that action comes BEFORE motivation, and then more action follows, then more motivation. . . .

Action comes Before motivation.

If you have to write a letter and can't get motivated, scribble an idea for the letter on a napkin. That small piece of "action" gets you going. Now you have started! Once you are in the middle of a task, there is a certainty that it's doable without major pain, and it's this certainty that you're onto a winner that makes you enthusiastic. To further build on this motivational seed, visualize yourself having finished the task. If you're really stuck on the first action step, find a motivating song and dance around the kitchen to it, or find someone who excites you about your project, and act silly with them on the phone. If this doesn't work, refer to "Always Making Excuses," earlier in this chapter. Remember a time when you were all action; act as that person again.

Discouraged

You've been knocked down, and you don't want to get up again. You've been turned down for a job you thought you were perfect for, and don't feel like applying or looking for another. You feel criticized, rejected, overlooked, and you don't want to put yourself through that pain again.

So what do you do? Retreat to a distance of fifty million miles and lick your wounds until you fall into them? NO.

Realize that doing nothing will mean ultimate pain— same old job or no job at all. You need to charge up your emotional, physical and mental batteries once more. Trust that it will happen, take a short break to breathe and reassess, and then move on.

Acknowledge what you've already done well, then think of how this wouldn't have happened if you'd given up when you first got discouraged. Remember and praise yourself for the positive results you've had in the past.

What are you good at? Tennis, cooking, computers, listening, singing, driving, sailing, dressing, leading, painting, helping? Spend some time doing that to reactivate your self-esteem. Tell yourself how good you are at it, and realize your power. This power can be used to enhance that area in which you feel discouraged.

Trying is part of the game. Just because it doesn't happen immediately doesn't mean it's not going to happen. If you'd given up on reading with the first difficult word you came across, or even the fifth or the thousandth, you wouldn't have learned enough to read this book. But you never gave up. Don't give up now.

It's the same formula. You knew you would one day read, so now be aware that one day you will get that

Remember and praise yourself for the positive results you've had in the past.

dream job, but only if you keep going. Identify anything you could be doing better or differently, and do it immediately.

Depression Dip

We're talking about the blues here, not long-term or clinical depression. If you are seriously depressed for a moderate or long period with no obvious reason, you must see a doctor and make sure they take it seriously.

Depression can also be a habit; we get used to feeling bad. Believe it or not, depression does something good for us (every bad habit has a good intention).

What do we get out of it? We get to talk about our feelings; we get love; we get attention. It may seem easy to get a sympathetic ear, but sometimes people just listen, or appear to listen, out of obligation and deep down do not appreciate being put in that position. It creates an excuse for not doing and an excuse for not dealing with or confronting certain people or situations in our lives. Depression gives us permission to shut down and not be ourselves, because being ourselves is too painful at that time.

So how do you dance out of the dip? First, realize that the very best way *out* is always *through*.

Identify the real reason or reasons for your depression:

~ You've been hurt by someone.
~ You feel your life is going nowhere.
~ You owe a lot of money.
~ You don't have many friends.

Depression can be a habit.

~ You have loads of friends, but you just don't like them.

~ You feel you're getting old.

~ You just ate that chocolate cake all on your own.

~ You don't have a car.

~ You don't have a date for Saturday night.

~ You don't have digital TV.

Yeah, right, like you needed us to give you examples of things you might be depressed about, but it's important to see how to boil it down to the particulars.

Now, don't focus on the problem, focus on the way out. What can you do to get yourself to a place that you won't want to escape from, a place where you feel good? What practical action can you take on the above difficulties?

Don't focus on the problem, focus on the way out.

TASK

1. Take three minutes to scribble down all the things that are contributing to your downer, then write up plans for turning them around. It's almost impossible to be taking positive action and still feel depressed.

2. You can also work on yourself in a direct way. Notice your posture, gestures and expressions when you're feeling low. Now remember your posture, gestures and expressions from when you were feeling great, and realign yourself with this

better-feeling body. Simply sit up straight, smile, breathe, move with energy, stand with confidence, with feet firmly planted on the ground (no limp gestures, no more spaghetti arms), open your mouth and say something positive out loud. Your mind doesn't know your body is just preempting the good feeling, and it will soon join in with feeling fantastic. Smile and laughter therapies are very popular, as people realize that smiling can trigger the happy feeling; it doesn't have to be the other way around.

3. Get a "happy outfit" if you don't have one already. Make it something that makes you feel on top of the world. It might be a bright, snuggly sweather and khakis for the guys, or a bright red dress with Audrey Hepburn sunglasses for the women (or vice versa!).

Get a
"happy outfit."

Remember that body, mood and outlook are all inextricably linked. Change even one, and the others can follow.

Substitution

Great! Fantastic! You've cleaned the kitchen! Well done. But you know that you did it rather than hitting a really vital task like answering those letters or cleaning the truly disgusting living room.

"Easy stuff first" usually ends up being "easy stuff only."

You substitute the big, difficult job with a smaller, easier one. You don't need to feel guilty, because you've still achieved something, but really you've just given yourself hyper-qualified reasons for not getting on with the Whopping Great Difficult Chore. OK, so you're not just watching TV or hanging out down at the diner, but this substituting is a habit that can lead to you achieving smaller, less significant goals rather than the larger ones. Substitution is a sly one, because you seem to be doing something positive and productive, but really you're just procrastinating under a prettier umbrella.

Maybe instead of knuckling down to those ultra-urgent letters, you suddenly find you simply have to rearrange your office.

EXAMPLE

Look at this list:

- ~ Ask for a pay raise.
- ~ Phone your aunt.
- ~ Write a presentation.
- ~ Take up a collection for someone's birthday.
- ~ Call a client back.
- ~ Make a dental appointment.

Decide what is important versus what would be easy to do and would make you feel good. Write numbers beside each task to show the importance of each. In the above example, number one might be, "Ask for a pay raise," and number six might be, "Phone your aunt." Do the important stuff first, no excuses.

Do the important stuff first.

Relapse

You are going gangbusters, then out of the blue your standards or your results seem to be sliding. You're getting less done, feeling less excited and generally slipping back to where you were before you began to make your life a gazillion times better.

You had set a great goal: doubling your sales by the end of the year. After having spent time on track to achieving this, an accident at work, an increasingly negative mindset, changed circumstances, a blippy economy, difficulty in a relationship or general burnout caused the good momentum to falter. You are off target in spite of your best efforts.

If you don't nip this in the bud, you could finally undo all your good work.

Relapse is inevitable, so don't beat yourself up over it, but you do need to take action, fully explore the circumstances and, if necessary, change tack.

To minimize slippage, review your goals and plans at least every couple of weeks. External circumstances are constantly changing, and in order to stay on your path, you've got to be flexible and ready to restrategize.

Review your goals.

Ask yourself this: Has the goal changed, or has your path to that goal changed? Do you still want to double your sales, or do you need to change the way you're going about it?

Imagine you're trekking through the jungle on the way to the buried treasure, using a great map that has served you well, and unexpectedly you come across a mountain not marked on the map. Do you climb the mountain or blast a hole through it so as to keep on course? Or do you bitch about the map and return home feeling defeated? Or do you draw a path around the mountain and follow that?

Awfulizing

This is when you turn on your drama queen. It's not that the boss was having a bad day and gave you a funny look—oh, no, that would be far too mundane to be *your* life.

In your head the boss shot you an evil look to let you know that you're a useless employee who's on the way out and was never any good in the first place. So it's all true. Not only are you a bad partner and a useless parent, but now there's living proof that you're no good at your job—and you always knew the boss didn't like you anyway.

Awfulizing is when you take any situation, positive, neutral or negative, and run it under the "terrible tap." You turn a manageable event into a volcanic eruption in your mind, spewing up the most hideous interpretations and outcomes.

Stop before you turn all life's roses into nettles. Do you know someone who does this all the time?

The difficulty you have is in your perception of the event, as opposed to the event itself. You must get up and get practical and see things as they really are, rather than in a way that your negative voice would be more comfortable with. Or at least confess that the state of affairs might not be as awful as your reality would have it.

When we blow things out of all proportion, we get emotional, and our judgment becomes even more vague and irrational. It's great to be creative, but only when it serves you for the better. It's time to move forward to choices. Do you want to feel bad or feel good? Make that decision. Remember what you did to improve your breathing and general physiology previously. Do it again!

Reality Check

Maybe the boss hates you, but what concrete evidence do you have for this? None? What about that look? It could mean something bad; it could mean nothing at all. You don't know, so why opt for the negative? Why select the option that is guaranteed to make you feel bad? Always ask yourself the question: Do I know that for a fact?

Do I know that for a fact?

Warning! Your life might be a little less tumultuous after this!

Not Phoning, Not Writing, Not Having the Conversation

You might be tempted to substitute any of the above three tasks for any of the others. However, it's vital for you to work out the most appropriate means of communication to achieve your desired outcome. These days, people tend to send off the difficult stuff in an e-mail rather than phoning, to break up with someone by phone rather than face-to-face and to schedule an unnecessary meeting rather than taking the time to draft a well-structured letter.

The All-Purpose Phoning Trick

Sex up your phone. Buy a phone that looks like James Dean or a winking Betty Boop. Make it a friendly and inviting place to go. Alternatively, stick silly messages all over your regular phone, saying, "I want you" or "You cute thing!" or anything that will make the phone a less daunting instrument. Antique phones can make you feel more composed and elegant; racing car phones can make you feel younger and more dynamic. It's all about setting it up so it's easier for you to feel great when you go to make that call.

- ~ Get clear on what outcome you want from the phone conversation. Mentally rehearse the best possible outcome. This will give you the necessary confidence to focus and follow through.
- ~ If you are finding a particular call difficult, either explain this to a friend, and have them sit with you through it, or make sure there is someone you want to impress in the room, as this way you'll automatically make yourself sound more impressive. Either way, you'll be damn pleased with yourself for having done it.
- ~ Think about the last time you made a call and felt fantastic. Make it happen again immediately.

- Don't let yourself do anything until you have made the call so that boredom will push you to it if nothing else.
- Reward yourself with a fun phone call for every three difficult ones.
- Return calls immediately so you don't have time to awfulize them.
- Look at the size of the phone, and compare it to the size of you.

If you have gotten yourself into a real state about making phone calls, try to interrupt your negative pattern by:

- Moving the phone to a different place.
- Standing if you normally sit.
- Dialing with a pen, pencil or chopstick.
- Dialing with the dial pad facing upside down.

The All-Purpose Letter-Writing Trick

Have all your stationery neatly ordered. If you're e-mailing, have a separate document in your computer for preparing e-mails so as to eradicate time stress when composing online.

- Scribble it roughly first. Just get your thoughts down on paper or screen—whichever you're comfortable with—regardless of what format the finished letter will be.
- Set yourself a time in which you want to achieve the result—five minutes, ten minutes, thirty

minutes? Is morning, afternoon or evening a better time to write it? A letter to a friend might be more suited to a long evening stretch, and a business letter to that five minutes before your coffee break. Be careful not to see this as an excuse to procrastinate.

~ Ask yourself what you need for the task: peace and quiet, inspiration, or a cowriter?

~ Write only what you want to say, rather than pandering to what you think a letter should be like.

~ Gather any outside information you may need ahead of time.

~ Address and stamp the envelope before you even write the letter, to make it a done deal.

~ Ask yourself if you're being too much of a perfectionist.

~ Ask yourself how you can make it simpler and more enjoyable to do (enjoy a big mug of hot chocolate as you write?).

~ Ask yourself how you'll feel when it's done.

~ Ask yourself how you'll feel if you wake up tomorrow with the task still hanging over you.

~ Ask yourself how you are going to reward yourself when the letter is written and mailed.

~ Get into a good letter-writing habit by writing nonessential letters, maybe to an old pop star flame, or sounding off to a politician or news-paper. Or get involved in letter writing for Amnesty International and know that your new ability is really making a difference in the world.

~ Realize that you could have written the letter in the time it took to read this troubleshooting section.

The All-Purpose Having-the-Conversation Trick

~ Write down the supposed difficulty with having the conversation.

~ Is it the reaction or the result you are nervous about?

~ Is it an emotional or practical difficulty?

~ Who is it going to affect, you or them? And how?

~ Who do you think you are protecting by *not* having the conversation? You, them or an outside party?

~ What do you think you're afraid of? Ridicule, rejection, loss of values, loss of something material?

~ It's vital to pinpoint the fear so you can break it down into manageable parts.

For example, if you need to have a conversation with your child's teacher, you might be afraid the teacher will criticize you for the way you're raising him or her. This fear can be broken down further to a fear of condemnation.

Now you can turn this around by making a decision not to react emotionally should the teacher criticize you or your children. Decide first that you are happy with your parenting, or if not, then address this separately. Then decide that you want something other than to feel bad. Set a positive agenda for the conversation ahead of time. Resolve that the result of the conversation will be knowing how your children are doing in class, how their social skills are, and how you and the teacher can work together for their happiness. In other words, know what you want rather than what you don't want.

~ Realize that you'll come out of it alive.

~ Choose to be concerned about what the other person is feeling in order to take the focus off yourself.

~ Don't take yourself so seriously. Find a way to have a laugh.

~ If you're feeling really uncomfortable during the conversation, realize that you're not stuck there but can walk out or reschedule at any time.

~ Arrange something to look forward to afterward.

~ Allow yourself time to have the conversation rather than rushing to get it over with. Slow down your speech, pause to think and notice the other person's reaction.

~ Acknowledge and compliment people so there's a good feeling to your conversations.

~ Ask people questions. People love to talk about themselves—this is the best chat oil in the world.

~ Be genuine. No one can ask you to be more than you are, and what you are is plenty good enough.

~ Check out your habits. If you meet socially, is
it in a noisy bar? Are you bending your elbow
too quickly with the whiskey? Are you blowing
smoke into your companion's face? Some places
and practices are not conducive to good
conversation.

~ As you walk away, congratulate yourself for
doing your best.

~ Don't do an autopsy on each awkward conversation afterward. Let it go. This will make the
next one easier.

Lack of Self-Confidence

~ You know what you'd like to do, but you feel
that you don't have what it takes.

~ You're nervous and hesitant before you com-
mence something that you have already decided
you want to do, to the point of stalling or
cancelling that which you know will be good
for you.

~ You might lack confidence socially and not
approach new people.

~ You might lack confidence in your ability at
work and about your career prospects, and fail to
try for a promotion

~ You may experience a lack of confidence in other
areas of your life—you may be feeling not quite
good enough in forming and maintaining long-
lasting and meaningful relationships.

Identify the Trigger

For most people, lack of confidence has a trigger, so try to identify what triggers you. If you don't overcome it, it can get worse:

- Are you eating well, getting sufficient sleep and regular exercise? All these can affect your confidence levels.
- If someone has criticized you, realize that it's their issue—they may envy you and wish they were as amazing as you are. Are you going to let them decide how you are feeling and what kind of person you are? If someone was to offer you a vast amount of money for acting unconfident for the rest of your life, would you take that money? No? Then why do it for free?
- We all revisit old feelings of inadequacy from time to time, but we can't stay there, so leave that place quickly and firmly, and move forward into self-confidence (you've been there before, too, you know!).
- Tell yourself that you can do it; it's not such a big deal. If anyone has done it in the past, then it can be done.
- Strike a pose. Create a superhero-type confidence pose—but don't wear your underwear over your pants, as this can create its own problems!
- If your lack of confidence is a bad habit, realize that confidence is a skill, and you will excel at it the more you move out of your comfort zone

and keep putting yourself into new, challenging situations. The more you do, the easier self-confidence will be.

~ Congratulate yourself on how great you are over and over every day. Don't expect others to do this job; they probably won't.

Self-confidence is a thing you do, not a thing you are, which means you have control.

Full Circle

You have almost reached the end of this book, and we highly recommend that you go full circle and, when you are done, turn back to the first page. You will gain more and more from this adventure each time you visit it. If you find that you have skimmed through some pages because you felt you had heard it before, yet you are still repeating the same old habits, then GO BACK!

Thinking is not doing or achieving—it is simply a building block. There is no end to this rich and fulfilling project, because, remember, YOU are the project! To make this work you have to "happen," by living and acting your life "a gazillion times better" than ever before. This will contine throughout your life, creating more enjoyment, love and abundance as you go.

We feel genuinely honored to be part of your amazing journey and know that you can find all-inspiring ways to benefit from this book with friends and family. We hope that you do.

FINAL TASK

Grab a pen and a couple of pieces of paper and quickly scribble down all the major changes for the better that you have put into place since starting this book.

Include all your achievements, no matter how big or how small—the emotional, the behavioral (noticeable to yourself or to others or both) and the practical.

- ~ What improvements have you made in your relationships with your family, lover, coworkers, friends and strangers?
- ~ What changes have you made to ensure that you are healthier and more energized by eating better and exercising more frequently?
- ~ How have you ensured that you earn your living by doing something you are passionate about?
- ~ What strategies have you put in place to ensure that wealth is flowing into your life?
- ~ In what other ways have you added to the quality of your life?
- ~ How are you contributing more in society?
- ~ What have you done for someone else lately?

You might like to draw the life-wheel again to get a visual representation of your progress.

Ask yourself the following questions, now and every day, talking them over with someone close to you whenever possible:

1. Who in my life is closer to me now?
2. What am I really excited about achieving today?
3. What wonderful things am I creating in my life over the next year?
4. How much better will my whole life be in five years' time?
5. What one thing can I do right now to pass what I have learned on to someone else?
6. How am I making the world a better place?
7. What am I grateful for in my life?
8. How can I have fun doing even more to make my life "a gazillion times better"?

Sometimes people forget to take time to congratulate themselves on their astonishing triumphs and accomplishments, so we'd like you to stand up and give yourself a huge round of applause and a pat on the back, as we applaud you also, because not only does it takes guts and a desire to be better than you were, but it also takes courage.

CONGRATULATIONS, YOU'RE MAKING IT!

Up, Up, and Onward

OK, let's crank this up to the next level! Already your vision is becoming reality, so make it stick! You have what it takes; you know that, and you're proving it every day. You owe it to yourself to make sure this doesn't turn into one of those books you get a couple of good ideas from and then let fall to the wayside and never pick up again. Right now, at this moment, you can make a difference in your life. Consistent action, even when you don't feel 100 percent great, is what will get you to where you truly desire to be.

It would be impossible for us to come to your house every day and power talk you into those emotions that are getting you there—excitement, commitment, joy, enthusiasm, passion, peace, creativity, zest and all those hundreds of other great feelings. More than anything, it is something you can do yourself and feel great about. It's your responsibility to talk and move yourself into those feelings every day.

Many people blame their environment for their lack of progress, lack of action, lack of good feeling (believe it or not, even after reading this book!). We've got news for you: your mind is strong enough that you can influence your environment; it doesn't have to be the other way around. Make every day a day in which you win out over any negativity that may be happening in or around you.

Here are some ways to ensure that what you've already put in motion is reinforced and continues to swell, grow and flow.

It's obvious by now that change doesn't happen in a vacuum; the whole world is swayed by what you do. Notice how the great new things you are implementing are affecting other people. If you sense that your developments are impacting those close to you in a negative way, beware that you could easily be tempted to revert back to your old behavior (within all of us resides that anything-for-a-quiet-life gene). We feel discouraged by negative feedback; we feel rewarded by positive feedback. We're all pre-programmed to interpret circumstances in this way. If you feel that what you are doing is benefiting others, and they are reacting positively to you, this will promote even greater upward momentum, and the people around you will follow. Bear in mind that sometimes you can be effecting change for the greater good and still meet a wall of opposition. Don't let this put a halt to the great work.

Here's an example of what can happen.

Debbie has just finished reading *Your Life Only a Gazillion Times Better* for the first time and is on fire about her new, exciting life. She feels happy for no particular reason. She smiles a lot and seems to reframe things that before she used to feel frustrated about. Her friend Billy used to talk to Debbie about his work problems and was comfortable with the ritual of meeting for a drink and complaining about his job to her. Now that she no longer wants to spend her time wallowing in what's wrong, Debbie gives him some tips on how to improve the situation. Feeling a loss of connection, Billy starts to get irritated with Debbie and cancels their next drinks night, causing her to feel tempted (because she values him as a friend) to slip back into their old way of relating.

On top of this, the women at work feel that she is trying to be better than them when she opts for salad while they go for the usual burger and fries. Debbie hears them whispering about her in the bathroom, sarcastically calling her "the super model" and saying that she always needs to be different, that she thinks she's above everyone else. Overhearing this, Debbie gets very upset and feels rejected and belittled, but she can't turn to Billy as she used to.

When she gets home, her teenage son is still sulking because the new family budget means that he can't have the very latest music system until all the credit-card debt is paid off.

So much for a better life! The people around Debbie are finding it hard to cope with the new things she has instigated. Learn from this typical scenario, and be sensitive to the fact that everything you do affects those around you.

Debbie has a choice: she could go back to her old ways, which were very comfortable and where she knew what to expect, or she can stay loyal to her new standards and find a better way of connecting with these people. This is what she decides to do.

She remakes the arrangement to meet Billy, and this time, when he complains about work, she listens for a while and then gently changes the subject. She decides to be nonjudgmental and understanding of his situation while not participating in his negative focus. Through telling him a story about how particular alterations she has made have been so beneficial to her, she invites him into her new perspective and then asks him questions about the accomplishments he would like to bring about in his own life. Making it clear that this is how she intends to continue living her life from now on, it becomes obvious to him how excited she is to be focusing on the positive and reaching her full potential. He feels inspired rather than threatened and sees himself as more involved in Debbie's life than ever before. She tells him that she would like to share this journey with him. If he insists on resisting a more productive way of behaving, it might be that she will have to see him less often for a while, or it might be that he becomes as enthusiastic about making life improvements as she is. Debbie is ready to accept either eventuality.

With the women at work, she decides to let their comments ride and continues to eat healthful foods. The most important thing she learns is that it isn't her job to revolutionize her colleagues' eating habits, nor is it their place to have Debbie conform to their norms. When it comes to lunchtime, she takes out her nourishing meal and makes light of it, smiling at their "rabbit food" jokes, and within a week they don't even notice that she's eating differently.

With her son, Debbie sits down and explains their financial situation, and they put together a plan whereby he can start to make money by doing extra chores beyond his normal household duties. This means that Debbie doesn't have to pay for outside help with the garden, and so on, and her son can start to have fun saving for the new music system. This not only helps their relationship, it also introduces him to a more responsible and realistic view of how money works, and helps him to create great values and habits for later years.

So, as you are swept up in this wonderful tide of enthusiasm, remember not to push your own agenda and remain respectful of other people's journeys and choices as you achieve. Being a self-help storm trooper is not what this is about. This is about making your life better in a holistic way.

This time of transition is only an adjustment period, and there will be many of these in your life, so relax and be comfortable with change. All it takes is some thoughtful communication and an extra drop of tolerance. There may occasionally be some confusion, and sorting this out is part of the fun and growth. Ask yourself: What will your attitude be during times of adjustment? Will you be confrontational and defensive, or playful, creative, and curious?

Who do you want to emulate? Rather than comparing yourself negatively to people or their opinions as to how you should be, set your own standard firmly and assert that standard all the time. Keep looking out for new people to model yourself after.

Who would it be a great idea to have as your role models in terms of health, career, wealth, spirituality, family and relationships? This is your team. Take note of who will be supportive and loving, and keep in contact with them weekly through their newsletters and books, and in person. Make sure you have a healthy mix of male and female energies to emulate. Bear in mind that people will also want to model themselves after you, so remain comfortable with this, and realize it doesn't mean they expect perfection from you. Lead by example rather than by dictating.

It is good, but not imperative, to have a buddy to travel this upward path with you. If possible, find someone who has the same, or higher, standards for how they want their life to play out. To keep in focus, have your friends as your friends, your lover as your lover, and your buddy as your coach. Hold each other to what you have declared you will get done. We often act as each other's buddies in this way, and it really works well. Schedule specific times to check in with each other.

What places will support you in your journey: the gym, park, library, seminar room, college, office, family room, kitchen, swimming pool, bookstore? Define what you want from each place and the emotions you want to feel while you're there. In the gym, perhaps you want to achieve a well-toned body and to feel energized and excited. Maybe you want to feel calm and relaxed in the park, to achieve an inner balance and connect with nature and friends.

What places do not support your journey: that chair in front of the TV, the neighborhood bar, a certain negative person's house, the candy store, untidy or dirty rooms, and unkept cars? Avoid or transform these places immediately!

What things will support you: collages, juicer, trampoline and other exercise equipment, tapes and books, journal, flowers, computer, cell phone, lucky charm, helicopter, devotional shrine, paintbrushes, a particular mug, perfume, a whole-food supplement, great clothes? Decide what things will make your life easier and surround yourself with them now.

Copy out some sections from this book onto Post-its, plaster them everywhere and use them as reminders for getting into great states for getting things done.

Make a special power-talk tape of your own voice saying the things that really get you excited. For example, "Today is my best day ever. I'm so excited about my life. I really look forward to taking the next steps. I am grateful for all that I have and all that I am. I can do it effortlessly. I feel great about who I am. I'm so happy that I'm healthy and wealthy. Today I am achieving my goals with joy and excitement." This stuff works, so work it!

The whole reason for becoming more consciously aware of what you're doing and making better choices is so you can consistently develop, contribute, and feel great in long, medium, and short term, in all areas. What is important is the person you become, a person who is constantly growing and marveling at life. Your life is about claiming what you deserve. If you can dream it, you can achieve it. The universe is conspiring to help you in every way, so realize there is a force greater than all of us powerfully assisting you in creating your dream-come-true.

There will be times you might feel stuck. Be good to yourself during these times, and realize that these rest periods are also part of the progress. An engine needs to cool in order to keep running efficiently, and these pit stops provide such great opportunities for enjoying the landscape around us. Time out is great, but make sure your rest period doesn't turn into a reversion to old habits. On this journey you will have up days and down days; sometimes you'll find yourself totally on target, and sometimes you'll be hitting wide of the mark. Either way, you are doing it, and you will get a result, eventually the very result you desire.

Take it from us, this stuff really does work. We have turned around our lives completely, and also helped thousands of others to do so. It's easy to make your life "a gazillion times better," so the next step is to continue improving. Simply know what your dreams are, know who you want to be, believe in yourself and go for it!

Further Reading

General

Andreas, Connirae, and Steve Andreas. *Change Your Mind—and Keep the Change*. Moab, Utah: Real People Press, 1987.

Bandler, Richard and John Grinder. *Frogs into Princes*. Moab, Utah: Real People Press, 1979.

———. *Transformations*. Moab, Utah: Real People Press, 1999.

McGraw, Dr. Philip C. *Life Strategies Workbook*. New York: Hyperion, 2000.

Robbins, Anthony. *Awaken the Giant Within*. New York: Simon & Schuster, 1992.

———. *Unlimited Power*. New York: Fireside, 1986.

Goal Fixing

Davidson, Jeff. *The Complete Idiot's Guide to Reaching Your Goals*. New York: Alpha Books, 1998.

Knaus, Dr. William J. *Do It Now*. Chichester, England: John Wiley & Sons, 1997.

Mind, Body, Spirit

Chopra, Deepak. *Ageless Body, Timeless Mind.* New York: Random House, 1993.

———. *Seven Spiritual Laws of Success.* Novato, CA: New World Library, 1995.

Hay, Louise L. *The Power Is Within You.* Carlsbad, CA: Hay House, 1991.

———. *You Can Heal Your Life.* Carlsbad, CA: Hay House, 1984.

Fun and Creativity

Cameron, Julia. *The Artist's Way.* New York: Tarcher/Putnam, 1992.

Jackson Gandy, Debrena. *All the Joy You Can Stand.* New York: Crown, 2000.

Relationships

Jeffers, Susan. *Opening Our Hearts to Men.* New York: Ballantine, 1990.

Norwood, Robin. *Women Who Love Too Much.* New York: Pocket, 1990.

Pease, Allan, and Barbara Pease. *Why Men Don't Listen and Women Can't Read Maps.* New York: Broadway, 2001.

Skynner, Robin, and John Cleese. *Families and How to Survive Them.* London: Oxford University Press, 1984.

Money

Allen, Robert G. *Multiple Streams of Income.* Chichester, England: John Wiley & Sons, 2004.